ARE WE NEARLY

Are We Nearly There Yet?

Wrestling with Issues in the Life of Faith

Gareth Evans

YOUCAXTON
PUBLICATIONS

ISBN 978-1-914424-97-7
Published by YouCaxton Publications 2023

YouCaxton Publications
www.youcaxton.co.uk

To all people of faith and to those who struggle with it.

Acknowledgments

I have a few heartfelt thanks to people who have supported and helped me with this book. To my wife Janette for her tremendous support as I worked on it and for her encouragement throughout. To my brother Gwynfor who read my first and second drafts providing advice and suggestions and without whose help this book would not have happened. To my sister Delyth for her tireless proofreading and editing.

To my children Tom, Jim and Kathryn who have always been there to challenge my long held views and who have helped me to widen my thinking. And to Kathryn, additional thanks for designing the book cover.

To Bob Fowke of YouCaxton Publishers for his support and guidance with the publishing of this book.

To many friends, too many to number for your patience and willingness to discuss many of the issues covered in this book. Your views have undoubtedly helped to shape mine.

To Michael Carding, Ian O'Reilly and Bruce Lawson for their help and advice along the way.

Contents

Introduction

'Are we nearly there yet?' That was the persistent and oft repeated question as we went on a car journey to our holiday destination when our kids were young. I'm sure many of you have heard the same. 'Not quite', was the reply, 'it won't be long. We're nearly there!' We would have played every game of *I Spy*, listened to every Roald Dahl story cassette (yes, I did say 'cassette', it's that long ago) and still the cry would ring out from the back seat, 'Are we nearly there yet?' Eventually we did of course get there, with three very bored kids in tow.

All of us are on a journey, a journey through life. As Christians we're also on a journey, a journey of faith. There are two ways I believe that we are on that journey.

The first is our journey towards whatever awaits us after we leave this mortal life. As Christians we are on a journey to Heaven, whatever or wherever that may be. Part of orthodox Christian belief is that there is an afterlife where we will go when we die. This life here on earth is not the end. We profess to know this with certainty, although many of us, if we're being honest, are uncertain what form this may take.

The second journey, and the one that I want to talk about in more detail, is how our faith develops and maybe changes as we progress on our faith journey. All of us who call ourselves Christian at some point had a starting point for our faith. For some that would be a date and time that is forever etched into their brains. Because of what happened in an experience of becoming aware of God they will never forget that time. For others, who grew up in the faith as part of a Christian family, they may struggle to be able to give a specific time or date. They would have been part of a church since before they could remember and were nurtured in the faith. At some point, assuming they stuck with it, that faith would become real for them, but that may have been a gradual process and they couldn't be specific on date, time or place.

I would count myself amongst the latter category. My earliest memories of church are at the Welsh Presbyterian Church in Oswald Road, Oswestry. We attended church as a family every Sunday morning and then Sunday school in the afternoon. The Minister was a lovely man called Pryce Williams and I still remember going down to the front of church to sit on the front pew and hear the 'Children's Address'. I recall one of his addresses when he talked about Airline Companies. At that time two of the biggest were BOAC and BEA. He used these letters to get his message across which was, 'Be on a course', and 'Be ever alert'. I've never forgotten that, although I have not followed it carefully one hundred percent of the time! Before the wonders of the children's address we all had to turn around to face the congregation and recite a Bible verse from memory. That is also my earliest memory of nerves. The kids who had managed to memorise the longest verse got the most praise from the gathered congregation, but as the verse memorising was invariably left till very late the day before, there was always the stock choice of John 11:35, 'Jesus wept'. My brother doesn't think that my recollection of the stock response verse is correct, and suggests that maybe the go-to verse was, 'God is love'. However, he can remember our mum saying how, when I recited Romans 12:18, it came out with a slight change to the Authorised Version: 'In so far as it lieth in you, live at peace with all *women*'.

Many people of my generation had a similar experience to mine, but in teenage years many drifted away from church, or indeed made a conscious decision to leave. When the option to go to church was up to them rather than a diktat from their parents, they made the choice to stay away and do something more interesting, like have a lie in on Sunday morning! That's not something I did. I stuck with it because for me, faith was starting to become a more personal experience. Through my teenage years and into my twenties when I left home and moved away for work purposes, I remained in the faith. My first move away from Shrewsbury, which was by now the family home, was to Ross-on-Wye and apart from finding a flat to live in, my two most pressing priorities were to find and join a church and a rugby club, although not necessarily in that order!

As life continued into marriage and a growing family, church was always an important part of my life and my faith in God an integral part of who I was.

Whichever route to faith we take, our journey is of a faith that develops. The way that you would suppose this happens is of a continuum of gradually deepening faith in God, with a growing understanding through prayer and reading the Bible. As we get to know more Christian people who become friends, you would suppose that doubts recede and faith in God takes on more certainty and that you eventually arrive at a position where you have no doubts about what you believe, and that matters of doctrine just fall into place. This is the faith journey that I'm talking about, the journey through discovery, study, fellowship and prayer. A journey that leads us to a place of certainty where no doubts exist, or perhaps are allowed to exist. Unfortunately, or perhaps fortunately, I have found that quite the reverse is in fact the case.

The problem is that the more you learn about our faith and the Bible, the more it raises issues, which to be frank, are not always that easy, or indeed possible to resolve. The more people you meet who have a Christian faith, the more versions of 'the truth' you come across. The nature of a faith experience is that it makes some people very certain about what they believe and it extends beyond the core beliefs of Christianity into matters of doctrine and morality. The problem is of course that when one person's certainty comes up against another person's certainty, a clash of beliefs is bound to happen. And that's just within the Christian faith, let alone other faiths.

My faith journey has brought me to a wonderful church now, in Meole Brace, Shrewsbury. I'm not a great lover of labels, but I suppose if you had to label our church it would be classed as evangelical, within the Church of England. Some years ago I felt a calling to consider training to become a reader in the Church of England and that is what I now am. 'Reader' - a wonderful term isn't it? For those not familiar with the office of Reader, it is an authorised ministry within the Church of England to lead services, preach and be part of the ministry team of the local Church. As part of my preparation for licensing as a Reader, I undertook three years of training. To be brutally honest it wasn't that enlightening a period of training and I believe that they have now made massive strides to improve this. I wouldn't say that it gave me that much opportunity to study theology, as would be the case for those training for ordination, so I certainly wouldn't consider myself theologically trained in any significant way. For this reason, the views expressed in this book are those of someone who wouldn't claim to be a theologian.

Some years ago I began to have some niggling thoughts and doubts about a few aspects of my faith. It started with reading the Bible. The evangelical view of the Bible is that it is the authoritative word of God, infallible and inerrant. The problem with this view is that as you read the Bible it throws up all kinds of problems, which are not easy to reconcile with what I and others have come to recognise as the character and nature of God. More of that in chapter one, but suffice it to say that it was causing me a big problem.

I was also getting to feel very uncomfortable about how my fellow Christians looked on people of other faiths. John 14:6 quotes Jesus as saying, 'I am the way, the truth and the life. No one comes to the Father except through me.' That has been taken to mean that unless people come to a faith in Jesus and renounce any other route to finding God, then they were condemned to Hell, whatever that is. And that, folks, is for eternity. The same goes for those of no faith and those who have had the opportunity to hear the Gospel but have rejected it. But what about people who have never had the opportunity to hear the Gospel? What about people who don't have the mental capacity to make that commitment? What about children who sadly die before they are able to make that commitment? What about people who are born in countries where the predominant religion is other than Christianity?

And then there is the issue of morals. Christians have long held very strong moral views on a whole plethora of subjects, largely based, at least originally, on particular interpretations of the Bible. These range from the use of alcohol, sexuality, the role of women, the distribution of wealth. The problem here is that our morals have evolved and changed in our society, some undoubtedly for the better. But as Christians we seem determined to draw red lines which cannot be crossed, even though society has crossed some of those lines years ago. Across the Christian Church there are now big variations on views on certain moral issues, and it's causing rifts. Those who are determined that all these red lines shall not be crossed, are so adamant on the subject that heels are dug in and the issues become almost fundamental to their beliefs, whilst those who have been happy to cross a red line or two are considered 'beyond the pale'. Can't we agree to disagree? Apparently not. And that was causing me some problems.

Another big one is the small matter of Jesus' crucifixion, why it happened and what was God's plan in all this. The basic evangelical take on all this can be summed up as follows:

- God made humans in his own image, but we messed up and sinned big time.
- God couldn't let all this sin go unpunished, so
- the consequence was eternal damnation.
- The only way to escape this was that someone had to be punished for all this sin.
- God sent Jesus to take the punishment on all our behalf.
- God sent Jesus to the Cross to die instead of us.
- God was 'satisfied' that the penalty had been paid, and
- if we confess our sins and accept Jesus as our Saviour we are forgiven and receive eternal life.

The theological term for all of this is 'Substitutionary penal atonement'. Having accepted this as an essential part of my faith for many years, it was starting to cause me a problem. Would God really do that? Is it actually in His nature to do so? If He tells us to forgive freely, why is He not able to do that Himself? As I was wrestling with this problem, I found out that I was not alone, and that many others, including renowned theologians, were asking the same questions.

And as these issues starting swirling around in my brain, other issues also rose to the surface. Does God really have a detailed plan for my life? Why does He, at least based on the evidence we see, not answer all our prayers? Why does He allow suffering?

The more I started wrestling with these issues, the more it made me feel that I shouldn't be thinking this way. Wasn't I questioning God? Wasn't I doubting Him? If I started actually rejecting parts of what had become core parts of my faith, what would I be left with? I was worried that I would unravel the whole fabric of my faith and be left with nothing. So I tried putting these problems to the back of my mind. I tried to reason with myself that there are some things we don't fully understand and that's the nature of faith. 'Don't slide', I told myself, 'or you'll be left with nothing'.

And then I tried asking people who I thought may be able to provide answers to my questions. People with serious theological training, people who were experts and would know how to put my mind at rest. Unfortunately, they didn't provide the answers I was looking for. Sometimes they confessed that they too had doubts and concerns about these issues. Or they were content not to know the answers. They trusted God and whereas there were areas that were baffling to them, they would leave it to God to make it clear to them at some point in time, be that before the grave or after! Or they went on the defensive and insisted that whereas some of the issues raised were grey areas, it is as it is, and if that's what God decided should be in the Bible, we must accept it and get over our discomfort. Some even went on the offensive and told me I was on dangerous ground and must fall in line with God's revealed word and way of doing things. The danger of not 'preaching the Gospel' was very real and a mortal danger, of which I and others of my ilk, should be aware.

There was a bit of a watershed moment for me that made me decide I needed to do something to sort out all my faith issues. I had started reading a daily on-line Bible reading app that went through the Bible in one year. Each day there was a chunk of the Old Testament, some from either Proverbs or Psalms and then some from the New Testament. Someone who is well respected in the Church, and by the evangelical wing in particular, produced it. The advantage of that kind of app is that it covers the entire Bible and not just the bits that are more palatable and that we tend to concentrate on. There is a tendency to avoid the parts of the Bible that we find difficult to deal with. But as this app covered all of it, then the difficult parts couldn't be avoided. On the day in question the Old Testament part covered Numbers chapters 15 and 16, which covers two particularly grisly accounts.

The first involves a man who was caught picking up wood on the Sabbath, which is counted as breaking the Sabbath rule that you must not work on the Sabbath. Picking up firewood counts as work, so the man was taken to Moses who enquired of the Lord what should be done with this man. The Lord told Moses that the man must die, which was duly carried out in the prescribed manner of the day – stoning.

The second episode in this part of Numbers describes a group of the Israelites who rebelled against Moses' leadership, which meant that they were in effect rebelling against God's leadership because Moses was God's anointed leader. What happened to this group of people is that they were all in one tent and the ground opened up and swallowed them all and then closed up above them. They were in effect buried alive.

This is the moment I thought, 'This man will know how to explain all this.' What he said was that there are parts of the Bible that are hard to understand and we should concentrate on the bits we can understand. Arghhhh!

From that moment I decided that I needed to sort this out for myself. None of the 'experts' were providing me with the answers. So, I started reading. I was amazed to find a huge wealth of books that dealt with these very issues. The authors were people who had come up against the same issues and have very helpfully put together some amazing books that deal with these issues head on. I am indebted to authors such as Steve Chalke, Brian McLaren, Marcus Borg, Rob Bell, Nadia Boltz-Weber, Dave Tomlinson, Vicky Beeching, Sarah Bessey, Peter Enns, Rachel Held Evans, Richard Holloway and others that I am still discovering.

I'm not claiming that I now have all the answers.... In fact, I've found that that is one of the answers. We can't have all the answers, but it's fine to have questions. It's fine to question God and even to rant at him. Just read the Psalms to prove that this is the case. I have come up with some answers that have helped me though, and I will articulate some of them in this book.

I would say that the whole exercise, which is ongoing, has actually strengthened my faith in God. It's provided me with some answers and left me with other questions unanswered. As people read this book, they will disagree with some of my conclusions and that's fine. Just as I may disagree with some of their views, which is also fine. The God who created this amazing universe is beyond mortal understanding. We can only get an inkling of what God is like and we may all see different bits. What none of us should do is to claim that the bit that 'I get' should lead us to say that that is the whole revelation of God and that nobody else's views have any credence. We can all learn from, and help each other, but we can only do that if we are tolerant of those who take a different view to us and whose experience of the divine differs from ours.

So, if you throw your hands up in horror at some of things I write in here, I'm sorry. But please remember that this search is to enable me to draw nearer to God, just as all people of faith want to do. James 4:8 says, 'Come near to God and he will come near to you.' That's what we all want to do. And it's part of the faith journey that we are on. It's a journey that leads us to discovery and revelation. Join me on my journey, a journey that is ongoing.

Questions to consider
1. Draw your own faith line, indicating high and low points.
2. Do any of the struggles mentioned in this chapter ring true for you?
3. Have other Christians been helpful to you in your questioning?
4. Is faith in God undermined by asking questions?

1

The Old Testament

The Bible, it's the only place to start really, and we'll be thinking about the Old Testament, a source of much head scratching for many Christians. The Bible is the sacred book of Christians the world over. It's not so much a single book actually, as a collection of books. In the standard Protestant Bible there are 66 books, in the Roman Catholic Bible there are 73 books and in the Eastern Orthodox Church, 78. It's divided into the Old Testament, which pre-dates Christ and is therefore the Hebrew Scriptures, and the New Testament, which is post the birth of Christ and consists of 27 books. All the three Christian traditions agree on those 27 books.

It's a collection of history, law, wisdom literature, letters, poetry and prophecies. It records the relationship between God and the human race and purports to tell the history of the Earth from its creation to the spread of Christianity in the first century.

It was written over a period of around 1300 years. The earliest parts of the Old Testament were thought to have been written about 1200 years BCE and the latest parts around 165 years BCE. The New Testament was written in the first century CE.

The Old Testament has, broadly speaking, three sections. The first can be described as the Law, although it includes stories such as creation and the early days post creation. The Hebrew word for law is Torah and is covered in the first five books of the Bible. These books are also referred to as the Pentateuch and they are traditionally attributed to Moses. There is also the Prophets and this is the largest section of the Old Testament. The writings make up the rest and constitute the Psalms, Proverbs, various Wisdom literature and some historical accounts.

The New Testament consists of four Gospels that tell the story of Jesus. The rest is mainly made up of various letters from itinerant church leaders, communicating with the Churches that they established. I could go into more detail but I think that's enough to set the scene.

So how did all these books get pulled together into one book? Well, that's open to some debate, but from evidence that scholars have, it seems that, over a period of maybe up to 300 years, different church leaders and theologians debated which books belonged in the 'Canon', as the Biblical text is collectively known. Although the bulk of the editing ended in the late 300's there was still debate right up to the 16th Century as to what should be in and what should be left out. The church reformer Martin Luther, for instance, had issues with the Letter of James being included because it emphasised the role of 'works' alongside 'faith'. He famously called it 'an Epistle of Straw'.

If indeed Moses did write the Pentateuch, I'm sure he never guessed in his wildest dreams that his writings would be bound together with other books written over a thousand years later to make a sacred text, or 'Bible'.

But what actually makes the Bible truly amazing and set apart from any other ancient texts is the claims made by evangelical and fundamentalist Christians. It can be summed up in three words - authoritative, infallible, and inerrant.

Authoritative – Although it is accepted that the Bible was written by human hands, and many different ones at that, the claim is made that it is the inspired word of God. What that means is that God inspired the writers to write down what they wrote, as a result of his direct inspiration. This effectively means that it is claimed to be God's word and therefore has true authority. 2 Timothy 3:16 states: 'All scripture is God breathed.' At the time that was written there was no New Testament, so this refers to the Hebrew Scriptures, our Old Testament. When the Bible is read in many churches each Sunday morning, the reader, having completed reading the allotted passage, says these words, 'This is the word of the Lord.' What that means of course is that the words of the Bible carry absolute authority because they come from God, via human hands. So, any issue you need to resolve, all you have to do is just look up the Bible and it will give you all the guidance you need. It sets out the history of God's developing relationship with the human race. That history is therefore, by definition, accurately recorded. The Bible, it is claimed, has the last word on all moral issues and all matters relating to doctrine.

Infallible – The Bible carries absolute authority because it cannot be wrong, it is therefore infallible. That means that all it says on matters of faith and Christian practice is wholly useful and indeed true. Its infallibility means that it cannot make false or misleading statements. There cannot be any errors and it is therefore:

Inerrant – There are no errors, false statements, or contradictions.

But are those claims borne out in reality?

In this chapter I will deal principally with the Old Testament. I grew up hearing and indeed reading the Bible on a regular basis. I have learnt many verses to add to the few that I learnt as a child in Oswald Road chapel. I do truly love the Bible. I also believe that God speaks to people through the words of the Bible and this is indeed my experience. You may be reading a passage that you know well and have heard many times before, and yet as you read it you can see something that you've never seen before.

But for all that, the Bible is a challenging book to read. It throws up some really difficult questions. Did God really do that? Did He really say that? Did He really tell people to do that? Some people, having read the Bible and come across some of the difficult challenges, have concluded that this cannot be the 'word of God'. The problem for the Church is that all too often we sadly avoid dealing with these difficult passages. We pick and choose which passages to read, thus avoiding dealing with the problem head on. The Old Testament book of Joshua for instance has some particularly difficult passages, describing acts of wanton violence and cruelty. And yet it's possible to go through a sermon series on the book without so much as a mention of the problem that confronts the readers. The elephant in the room is frequently ignored.

I will go through some of the problems that the Bible throws up for us, problems that others, who would wish to undermine the message of Christianity, are all too quick to point out. They will point out passages which appear to contradict the image that we would wish to put forward of a loving God, a God who is just, cares for His people and hates inequality.

In his book *The God Delusion* the well known atheist Richard Dawkins describes the God of the Old Testament in this way: 'The God of the Old Testament is arguably the most unpleasant character in all fiction; jealous and proud of it; a petty, unjust, unforgiving control-freak; a vindictive, bloodthirsty ethnic cleanser; a misogynistic, homophobic, racist, infanticidal, genocidal, filicidal, pestilential, megalomaniacal, sadomasochistic, capriciously malevolent bully.'[1] That's pretty strong stuff. But why does he say all this? Well, the Bible does add some fuel to his argument, as we shall see.

So, what are these problems that confront us as we read the Old Testament? The following are the areas that I will deal with, although there may be more that others would highlight: the violence and killing; the laws; and historical accuracy.

Violence and Killing

The Old Testament is packed with many accounts of blood curdling acts of wanton slaughter and violence. What makes it disturbing is that the text makes it quite clear that this is at God's instigation. He either carried it out Himself directly or instructed others to do it. Books such as Joshua are packed with accounts of slaughter of men, women and children, and even animals.

The commentary that I have at home on the book of Joshua starts with the author stating, 'The stories of Joshua are among the most exciting in the Bible. Who has not thrilled to the drama of the march around Jericho and the collapse of the wall?'[2] I think I would want to add to that comment. Who hasn't wondered about the bloodshed and violence we read about and who hasn't puzzled about why it is that we are told that Joshua and his army carried out this grizzly task on God's instruction?

To illustrate the point, I will just discuss a few narratives, although there are many others that I could have highlighted.

Noah's Ark

For some reason this story is one of the favourites for children's Bible stories. Many a children's Bible story book has pictures of a quaint wooden boat with various animals going up the gangplank in twos. Quite why this is chosen as a go-to story for children I'm not quite sure as it basically deals with the fact that God got so fed up with people sinning and not making right choices that he decided to flood the whole world and drown everybody apart from one family, that of Noah.

And this is only six chapters into the Bible.

Genesis 6: 7-8: 'So the Lord said, I will wipe mankind, whom I have created, from the face of the earth – men and animals, and creatures that move along the ground, and birds of the air – for I am grieved that I have made them. But Noah found favour in the eyes of the Lord.'

It's not clear what all the animals, birds and other creatures had done to deserve this fate, but mankind had committed such wickedness that God decided that he should drown them all and start again. Two of each animal would be preserved on the Ark so that things could get off to a fresh start.

I will deal with the historical accuracy issue later, but this is an act of massive destruction of life. It is dreamt up and instigated by God. Is this the way that God deals or dealt with sin? Shortly after the Creation, God got so fed up with the wickedness of mankind that He decided to wreak this total global havoc. It was an act of massive loss of life and destruction. Ethnic cleansing on a global scale!

God punishes rebels

In Numbers Chapter 16 we read a story set in the time when Moses was leading the Israelites through the desert towards the Promised Land. Moses was God's appointed leader, so his authority came from God. To cut a long story short, some of the Israelites were having a go at Moses about his leadership and rebelled against him. How far that went isn't certain, but Moses complained to God about them and asked Him to 'sort them out'. God duly obliged. Moses said to the rebels that they were going to pay for their rebellion. We pick the story up at verse 31. 'As soon as he finished saying this, the ground under them split apart and the earth opened its mouth and swallowed them, with their households and all Korah's men and all their possessions. They went down into the ground, with everything they owned; the earth closed over them, and they perished and were gone from the community.' To add to that, the Lord then sent fire to consume 250 other men.

Again, pretty gruesome stuff, and carried out by God as a direct action, albeit at the pleading of his appointed leader. God buried people alive for complaining about Moses and how he was leading them.

Punished for picking up sticks

Immediately preceding this incident, in Numbers Chapter 15 we read of an incident that involved a man who was caught picking up wood on the Sabbath day. The important thing to remember here is that picking up wood was classed as work, which was forbidden on the Sabbath. The man was brought to Moses and Moses was asked what they should do with him. God intervened at this point and told Moses that the man must die. So, the assembly took the man outside the camp and executed him in the prescribed manner, which was stoning to death.

So, we have moved now to another aspect of the killing and violence. Here it is carried out by people, albeit under the guidance given to the Israelites by God and the Torah (the laws given to Moses by God).

The Book of Joshua

After 40 years wandering through the desert, Moses led the Israelites to the verge of crossing into Canaan, the Promised Land. He died before he could lead the people into the Promised Land and Joshua took over as leader. The book of Joshua gives an account of how the Israelites fulfilled the promise of God to take over the land 'flowing with milk and honey'. It describes in detail how they swept all before them as a conquering army, wiping out whole swathes of the indigenous population as they went. Ethnic cleansing is not too strong a word to describe what happened.

The most famous victory in the book is that at the battle of Jericho where the Israelites blew their trumpets and the walls fell down, enabling the conquering army to march into the city, take it over and kill all its inhabitants. Well nearly all... A prostitute called Rahad and her family were spared because she had given some spies shelter and facilitated their escape when they came to spy on the city before the battle.

In chapter 6:21 we read that when the walls of Jericho fell, 'They devoted the city to the Lord and destroyed with the sword every living thing in it, men and women, young and old, cattle sheep and donkeys.' So that's children and babies included. Nothing or nobody was to be left alive, apart from the aforementioned Rahab and her family.

In my view it gets worse in Chapter 8 when they move on the campaign to the next place on the list, a city called Ai. Here the army use a different tactic to the trumpet blowing used in Jericho. Here they used military guile. Their army essentially set a trap by appearing to be running away from the army of the city. They retreated and once they did so, the army of Ai pursued them, leaving the city undefended with the old men, women and children unprotected. Once Joshua's army, or part of it had retreated far enough, they sprang the trap they had set with the remainder of the army and defeated their enemies, which of course meant putting them all to the sword. They then returned to the undefended occupants of Ai and slaughtered all of them - that's women, children and old men too old to fight in the army.

To say that it doesn't meet the standards of the Geneva convention on the actions in war is putting it mildly. And let's not forget that, although this was carried out by Joshua and his army, it was under the guidance and with the blessing of God, or so the text suggests.

As you read through the book of Joshua it is filled with more of the same, as the Israelites occupy the land promised to them by God.

It's interesting to note that when you consider the sad events in Israel and Palestine today, there are those who believe that Israel has the right, the God-given right, to occupy all of the disputed land because it was promised to them by God. This promise is set out in scripture and the promise was for all generations and therefore it cannot be questioned or altered because it is set out in the Bible, God's word, His infallible word. Just consider these few verses from the book of Psalms to illustrate the point:

Psalm 105:44: 'He gave them the lands of other peoples,
and let them take over their fields.'
Psalm 111:6: 'He has shown his power to his people,
by giving them the lands of foreigners.'
Psalm 135:12: 'He gave their lands to his people.'

You will have gathered by now that the basic way of doing battles was win, and then kill everybody.

Whilst Moses was leading the Israelites through the desert, he had various skirmishes with some people known as the Midianites. After Moses and his men had finally defeated their army, there is an account in Chapter 31 of the Book of Numbers, of how the conquering army had killed all the men and captured all the women and children and then came back to Moses to tell him how things had gone. We pick up the account at verse 15:

'"Have you allowed all the women to live?" he asked them. "They were the ones who followed Balaam's advice and were the means of turning the Israelites away from the Lord in what happened at Peor, so that a plague struck the Lord's people. Now kill all the boys. And kill every woman who has slept with a man, but save for yourselves every girl who has never slept with a man"'.

In a nutshell, virgins could be treated as spoils of war in that circumstance, but all the other women and boys had to be killed. Now I must confess that during my many attendances at Church over my life I may have nodded off on the odd occasion. However, I do not recall ever hearing that passage read in Church!

I could go on. These are just a few examples of the many passages in the Old Testament that describe gruesome levels of killing and violence. This includes, for instance, the account of the Exodus,

8

where God rescued the Israelites from slavery in Egypt. This episode includes God killing all first-born children in Egypt except the Israelites who were spared because they had daubed their doorposts with the blood of a Lamb, which was a symbol to the Angel of Death that he should 'pass over' this particular house in his journey of killing. This is the Passover, celebrated by Jews from that day to this.

All of it, on the face of it, is either carried out by God, or by His followers on his instructions. What are we to make of this? Well, there are various ways of dealing with it and possible explanations, but first of all let me turn to the other problem areas.

The Law

Much of the Torah, the first five books of the Bible, is taken up with Laws. There are 613 of them altogether and they cover all kinds of things from relationships, worship, farming practices, land ownership, how to treat your slaves and they also prescribe punishments for transgression of these laws.

They are attributed to Moses, albeit that they came to him from Yahweh. Yahweh is one of the Hebrew names for God used in the Bible. The most well-known of these laws of course are the Ten Commandments, which are fundamental in both Judaism and Christianity. They were revealed to Moses on Mount Sinai during the time when the Israelites were in the desert for forty years on their way to the Promised Land, having escaped slavery in Egypt.

Because of the nature of the culture in which they lived, the Law was both spiritual but also civil. The Israelites were obliged to obey the Law, and the religious leaders, right up to the time of Jesus and beyond, made it their duty and pleasure to ensure that everybody adhered to them. Regulations were interpreted rigidly and appear to us today as excessive.

Let's take for example the law against working on the Sabbath. That meant that you couldn't do any work at all. Jesus had a run-in with the Pharisees on several occasions regarding this law. When Jesus healed people on the Sabbath, he was criticised because this constituted work. When his disciples plucked ears of corn on the Sabbath in order to eat them, this also incurred the wrath of the Pharisees as this also counted as work. They saw this as harvesting and threshing, which were of course work.

The Laws were very detailed and prescriptive, and observation of them was considered essential to being in a right relationship with God. They were written around 8,000 years ago, so in spite of the fact that they are considered to be the inspired word of God, are they applicable to us in the 21st century? Well, on that there is much debate.

Frankly, some of them are a bit bazaar and we totally disregard them to all intents and purposes. An example of this is that it is forbidden to wear clothing made from two kinds of material (Leviticus 19:19). However, others are still quoted by those who wish to point out why a particular moral viewpoint should be considered the will of God. For instance, when it comes to debating the rights and wrongs of same sex relationships, Old Testament quotes are trotted out to supposedly prove that we stray from an erstwhile traditional standpoint at our peril. Few however would consider our souls to be in mortal danger if we wear clothing made of two kinds of material.

Dave Tomlinson, in his book *Re-enchanting Christianity,* quotes an anonymous letter posted on the internet some years ago. [3] It was addressed to Dr Laura Schlessinger, an American radio host. As an Orthodox Jew she had denounced homosexuality, citing a passage in Leviticus. The unidentified correspondent wrote:

> Dear Dr. Laura,
> Thank you for doing so much to educate people regarding God's Law. I have learned a great deal from your show, and try to share that knowledge with as many people as I can. When someone tries to defend the homosexual lifestyle, for example, I simply remind them that Leviticus 18:22 clearly states it to be an abomination ...
> End of debate.
> I do need some advice from you, however, regarding some other elements of God's Laws and how to follow them.
> 1. Leviticus 25:44 states that I may possess slaves, both male and female, provided they are from neighbouring nations. A

friend of mine claims that this applies to Mexicans, but not Canadians. Can you clarify? Why can't I own Canadians?

2. I would like to sell my daughter into slavery, as sanctioned in Exodus 21:7. In this day and age, what do you think would be a fair price for her?

3. I know that I am allowed no contact with a woman while she is in her period of menstrual uncleanliness - Lev.15: 19-24. The problem is how do I tell? I have tried asking, but most women take offense.

4. When I burn a bull on the altar as a sacrifice, I know it creates · a pleasing odour for the Lord - Lev.1:9. The problem is my neighbours. They claim the odour is not pleasing to them. Should I smite them?

5. I have a neighbour who insists on working on the Sabbath. Exodus 35:2 clearly states he should be put to death. Am I morally obligated to kill him myself, or should I ask the police to do it?

6. A friend of mine feels that even though eating shellfish is an abomination - Lev. 11:10, it is a lesser abomination than homosexuality. I don't agree. Can you settle this? Are there 'degrees' of abomination?

7. Lev. 21:20 states that I may not approach the altar of God if I have a defect in my sight. I have to admit that I wear reading glasses. Does my vision have to be 20/20, or is there some wiggle-room here?

8. Most of my male friends get their hair trimmed, including the hair around their temples, even though this is expressly forbidden by Lev. 19:27. How should they die?

9. I know from Lev. 11:6-8 that touching the skin of a dead pig makes me unclean, but may I still play football if I wear gloves?

10. My uncle has a farm. He violates Lev.19:19 by planting two different crops in the same field, as does his wife by wearing garments made of two different kinds of thread (cotton/ polyester blend). He also tends to curse and blaspheme a lot. Is it really necessary that we go to all the trouble of getting the

whole town together to stone them? Lev.24:10-16. Couldn't we just burn them to death at a private family affair, like we do with people who sleep with their in-laws? (Lev. 20:14) I know you have studied these things extensively and thus enjoy considerable expertise in such matters, so I'm confident you can help. Thank you again for reminding us that God's word is eternal and unchanging.

Your adoring fan.

Dave Tomlinson comments: 'The letter is good entertainment value. But it also makes a serious hermeneutical point: literalism makes a laughingstock of the Bible – clearly no sensible person can believe that God declares menstruating women unclean, or commands that disobedient children are stoned to death.'

There are also prescribed repercussions for failing to obey and follow all the laws and commandments. Deuteronomy chapter 28 deals with blessings for obedience and curses for disobedience. The first 14 verses details blessings you can rightfully expect as your reward for obedience and then a full 53 verses that warn you about the curses that will come your way for disobedience to God's commands. These include:

- being plagued with diseases,
- the Lord causing you to be defeated by your enemies,
- having Locusts devour your crops,
- having your knees and legs afflicted with painful boils,
- your sons and daughters being given to another nation,
- you being pledged to be married to a woman, but another will take her and ravage her.

The list goes on. You would think that a fine or short custodial sentence would be sufficient!

What are we to make of all this? Should we disregard it all? Should we accept it all as God's word for all time, or should we pick and choose? If we do that, how do we decide which bits to choose and which bits to disregard?

Historical Accuracy

One of the major discussion points about the Bible concerns the accuracy of what is written. Did the events happen just as they are described.... literally? Was the book written as an historical record? This is especially pertinent given that there are many different authors who did not confer with each other. If they were inspired by God to record this history, then it could follow that they wrote what they wrote in their own hand, but that a greater source of inspiration prescribed the words they wrote.

The question has to be asked at this stage as to whether it actually purports to be an historical book or books. Some argue that yes, it is intended to be taken as historically accurate. Others would argue that much of the script is metaphorical. As metaphor, much of the text could be considered to be like a work of art, such as a story or painting, in which the characters, images and events act as symbols. The authors may have been using story form to illustrate a moral or spiritual truth. As such, the parabolic writing, if that is what it is, can be understood to be a type of extended metaphor.

Of course, both can be considered useful for readers of the Bible. The point at issue is that those who insist that it is historically accurate treat this as a matter of principle and that to err from this viewpoint undermines the whole integrity of the Bible.

As I said previously, a good part of the Old Testament is taken up with wisdom literature, with prophecy and with hymns and prayers in the Psalms. There are, however, large sections which deal with historical records and purport to date back to Creation, and which chronicle the developing relationship between God and the human race through God's chosen people, the Israelites. This is from Creation up to the birth of Jesus Christ. This starts off with the accounts of Creation in Genesis 1 and 2. I say accounts because in these chapters there are two different accounts of creation. This is such a fundamental issue that I have devoted a whole chapter to this. The debate between Creationists and Evolutionists is still a massive issue, particularly in the USA, and is seen, wrongly in my opinion, as a battle between science and faith.

If the Old Testament is indeed historically accurate and factually correct in all respects, then this dates the events of Creation at less than 10,000 years ago. More of that in a later chapter, but what about some of the stories in the Old Testament? Are they accounts of actual events? I'm going to highlight just a few and consider if we can seriously take them as historical events, or whether we should take them as allegorical in their nature.

Noah's Ark, as I mentioned previously, is a go-to must for children's Bible stories. Although God is purported to have wreaked destruction on the human race, what about the actually story line? Can we take this literally?

Noah was told to take his family and two of every kind of living creature into the Ark, in order to preserve them for the future. The Ark that Noah built was of a size specified by God and it was to be 450 feet long, 75 feet wide and 45 feet high. This was presumably so that all these creatures could fit inside. Noah is chronicled as being nine generations after Adam and Eve. Even though some of the people in Genesis are said to have lived very long lives, because of the timeline that we are working to here, all this will have happened no more than 9,000 years ago. The reason I mention this is because if this account is accurate then all the animals roaming the Earth now will have descended from that pair of their forbears that went onto the Ark.

Scientists have recently estimated that there are approximately one to two million species of animals in the world today. The same study estimates that 86% of all land species and 91% of all sea species have not yet been discovered or described. Even allowing for the fact that some species are sub species, there is simply no way that two of all those species could have got into an ark 450 feet long. The text suggests this:

Genesis 7:15 – A male and female of every type of animal.

Genesis 7: 2 – 7 pairs of ritually clean animals, but just 1 pair of every ritually unclean animals!

Another interesting one to throw into the mix is that Noah was said to be 600 years old when he went into the Ark and lived a further 350 years after he came out of the Ark, making him the grand old age of 950!

Scientifically all this is impossible and even though God can do anything that He chooses, are we meant to take this literally? People, in an effort to justify this story, have unearthed records of great floods and the remains of a huge boat. But is this actually a myth? If it is, can we nonetheless take spiritual lessons from it in considering the way that Noah lived his life and that there are consequences when we get things wrong? I would say yes to this, and I would venture to suggest that if we try to convince people that this story is historically accurate, then we start to give ourselves a credibility issue. Furthermore, our faith in God through Jesus does not rely on us believing in this story as actual historical fact.

There are many other stories in the Old Testament which I could go into further detail about, but for our purposes now I will just list a few which I would question in terms of their historical accuracy, but from which we can learn much if we read them allegorically. These would include Jonah and the big fish, the Tower of Babel, the Exodus from Egypt and the parting of the Red Sea, Daniel in the Lion's Den and Balaam's talking donkey.

How do we deal with all this?

As I said in the introduction, for many years I had found these issues to be really challenging. I sought answers in many places and I have now started to find answers that, although leaving some questions unanswered, do at least enable me to move on in my journey with God. I do believe that many people over the years have found some of these problems to be so problematic that they have concluded that the Christian faith is not for them. Sadly, many will have sought answers from Christians who have given them various explanations that they found to be unhelpful.

So, what are the possible answers that people will point to as explanations for these issues?

God is Sovereign. The view is expressed that basically it's not up to us to decide how God should behave, or that He should fit in with our views as to how He should go about things. It's God's way not our way - get over it! The Bible says that the human race is created in the image of God, but can we be guilty of trying to turn the tables here and creating God in our image? The way we consider moral issues has changed much over recent years and is certainly very different to how things were when the Bible was written. But if God's way is how it is described in the words of the Bible, then it's not up to us to put onto God a standard that suits us now. We should accept the standards as set out in the Bible, which after all is the inspired word of God. Or should we?

The problem with that is that as Christians we have learned so much about the nature of God, through the person of Jesus Christ. That nature appears to be at odds with much of what we read in the Old Testament. When the religious authorities brought to Jesus a woman caught in the act of adultery, an offence punishable with death by stoning, Jesus didn't say, 'Yes, carry on and stone her.' He told them, 'He who is without sin cast the first stone.' (John 8:7) This is different to the edict given to Moses by God when the man was caught picking up wood on the Sabbath. He was to be stoned as prescribed by the law.

The New Testament script is not without challenges of its own, but the nature of God as we discover through Jesus does not appear to be, 'I'm sovereign - get over it!'

God's ways are mysterious. We don't fully understand God's ways, so we have to leave things we can't get our heads around as a mystery. God is by nature a mystery. We don't and can't possibly understand everything there is to know about God. If we could, He wouldn't be God. In the modern era we're not happy if we can't provide reasons and explanations for everything. Science has enabled us to do a great deal of that, and we now understand so much more than we ever used to. But the argument here goes along the lines that you can't know all things. God is a mystery, so you must leave some things as just that... a mystery.

To be fair, I've heard this argument a lot, as various people have attempted to provide me answers to my various niggling doubts. Yes, the violence in the Bible is a mystery, but let's leave it at just that, a mystery, to which we don't know the answer. I've had many a discussion with 'Bible-believing' Christians who struggle with many of the same things that I've struggled with and which I've articulated here. But faced with the choice of having to leave it as a 'don't know' and the choice of coming up with an alternative explanation which may have to include an answer which allows for the fact that God may not actually have said that or done that, they choose the former. To countenance the thought that the Bible may actually contain some things that are not, or never were God's will, then they have to leave it as a mystery, something they can't explain.

I do have some sympathy for this point of view. I held that view for some time myself, but the questions wouldn't go away. Why would God inspire people to write things that were problematic? Surely if God inspired the writers of the various books in the Bible, why would he inspire them to write things that were problematic for us? Why would he inspire them to write things that confused us? And so, I discounted this explanation in the main part, knowing that in some way I had to reconcile the God I read about in the Old Testament and the God of love, who I worship as a Christian and have followed all my life.

They all deserved it. Some would argue that God had been patient with them for hundreds of years, but that He had finally had enough of their pagan ways. But surely God doesn't rid the world of people who don't worship Him?

And did the children and babies deserve it? I won't spend long on this argument because I don't think it merits much discussion time. The idea that God ran out of patience with people's sinful ways and therefore wiped them out, or empowered His favoured people to do it, just doesn't fit in with the character of God as we have come to know Him. Why doesn't He do it again and again every time we mess up?

Yes, it was bad, but God wasn't always like that. The argument goes that the Israelites were God's chosen people and that he was paving the way for those chosen people, a way that would eventually lead to the birth of Jesus. But again, the idea of a God that has favourites doesn't warrant a lot of discussion time, especially when that favouritism leads to wholesale killing and genocide for those who are not the favourites.

17

It was the olden days. This is how things were done then. God was participating in how people did things in their day and age. But why would God participate in something that is not part of His nature?

The start of a possible solution

I have to say that none of these possible explanations has helped me in my own search for answers to the questions. So where do we go for a possible explanation?

Let me say at this point that there has to be a place where we can ask questions. We should be encouraging people to ask questions, especially when the lack of answers can be a hindrance to their faith. We have to be in a place where people can hold different views and still be accepted with grace and love. I love the Bible. That's my starting point.

So that said, not everybody will agree with everything I am saying here. That's fine. If we are those who class ourselves as Christians, then we are brothers and sisters in the fellowship of Christ's Church. Let's have this dialogue as we wrestle with difficult issues.

So, what are the possible answers to these questions?

I think the first thing that we have to say is that the Bible always has to be read bearing in mind the context of the time that it was written.

At the time when the described battles took place, there was no Geneva Convention. There were no established protections for the wounded and sick, and for the civilians in and around a war-zone. If this had been the law when Joshua had been around, he would have been indicted as a war criminal for genocide and war crimes. But there was no such convention in his day. The way he did war was the way war was done.

This explanation does possibly start us on the path to understanding these issues.

That's how things were done then. So, it should be no surprise to see an account that describes it the way it was.

I've been very much helped in my thinking on this by the American Biblical scholar, theologian and author Peter Enns. He is one among many who have grappled with this issue. Others are Brian McLaren, Rachel Held Evans and Steve Chalke.

Peter Enns' take on this is not to dismiss these stories; they are after all part of the Bible. He says we should try to understand them.

The culture that prevailed at those times was very much a tribal culture. Peoples of different tribes and cultures had their own gods and worshipped in many different ways. They believed that God was their God and was basically on their side. So, it is natural that they would expect that, when it came to war, their God would be on their side and would give them victory over their enemies. And of course, the Israelites were no different and their writing would reflect that. They were depicting God in the way that they understood God to be. They were devoted to God and their writings reflected that devotion.

This is how Peter Enns puts it: 'The Bible shows us that obedience to God is not about cutting and pasting the Bible over our lives, but seeking the path of wisdom, holding the sacred book in one hand and ourselves, our communities of faith, and our world in the other in order to discern how the God of old is present here and now.' [4]

These ancient writers had an adequate understanding of God for their time, but not for all time. If we can accept that, we are in a much better position to accept these stories, and not try to whitewash the details and make up explanations to ease our stress.

So did God instruct Joshua to kill every living thing in Jericho and Ai? I would say an emphatic 'no'. But did Joshua think that that was what God was saying to him? Yes. These stories are written based on people's understanding of God at the time they wrote them.

Over the history of the Christian church our forebears have done terrible things based on what they understood the Bible to be telling them:

- When Wilberforce and others were waging a campaign against the slave trade, there were those in the Church who fought hard to retain it based on passages in the Bible, which on the face of it condone slavery.
- When the Black population in South Africa, supported by so many people around the world, were struggling to overcome

apartheid, there were Christian people putting a point of view forward that the Bible gave apartheid legitimacy.

- As women have fought for the right to exercise ministry roles within the church, there have been, and still are, people within the church who have argued that based on biblical principles these are roles that should be preserved only for men.
- There are those within the Christian church who would argue that, based on Old Testament passages where God promised the Promised Land to Abraham and his descendants, that the modern state of Israel has a God-given legitimacy to drive Palestinian people from their land and their homes.
- To this day, people are denied the opportunity for same-sex marriages in most churches, and homophobia is a real and persistent problem. This is all justified based on biblical text.

The history of humankind is one of development and change. We continue to understand things a little bit better with every passing age, and that will continue. Future generations will look back on us and wonder at some of the things that we are doing now in God's name, or at least what future generations will interpret as contrary to God's will:

- They will wonder at how we contrived to attempt to destroy the planet by a disregard for proper stewardship of the earth's resources.
- They will be amazed at how we allowed people to sleep rough whilst we were living in warm comfortable houses.
- They will wonder why the church hasn't yet agreed to same sex marriages. This is a debate that's playing out now of course and is based on passages in the Bible.

How are we to make sense of all this? The Bible and life as a whole for us, needs to be seen through the lens of belief in Jesus. In Jesus we see the nature of God. When asked what the greatest commandments were, he said:

- Love the Lord your God.
- Love your neighbour as yourself.

Perhaps we can take something of a lead from Jesus who on several occasions appeared to challenge some of these old Laws. As part of the Sermon on the Mount (Matthew 5:38) Jesus said: 'You have heard it said "Eye for eye, tooth for tooth", *but now I tell you*. Do not resist an evil person. If someone strikes you on the right cheek, turn to him the other also.' Jesus was quoting from Leviticus 24 which states 'If anyone injures his neighbour, whatever he has done must be done to him: fracture for fracture, eye for eye, tooth for tooth.' What was Jesus doing here? Maybe He was taking the Law of Moses to the next level. Not ditching it, but developing it. Or perhaps he was saying that this law doesn't apply any more. Either way He was telling them that they didn't need to follow that law as written. What else might this apply to?

On the occasion when Jesus was criticised for allowing his disciples to pick some ears of corn on the Sabbath, Jesus replied to them: 'The Sabbath was made for man, not man for the Sabbath.'(Mark 2:27) I think what Jesus is alluding to here is that the Laws were not written as a slavish set of rules to be adhered to, but laws that can benefit people in how they lived. The Sabbath as a day of rest is a great idea and people need to rest and have time away from the daily grind, and Sabbath rest enables that. This was in effect the first Trade Union legislation, giving people a rest from their back-breaking work.

Was Jesus actually saying there, well that's what they thought back then, that's what they thought God was saying then, but actually what you should do is this?

The Bible is a collection of books compiled over thousands of years that contains people's response to the reality of God. God's people have been on a journey in which we can see a development in their understanding of who God is - just as there has been in our own lives. It is in Jesus that we see the fullest revelation of the heart and mind of God.

The Old Testament as a God-breathed text

So, given all that I have said here, is there still a way for us to read the Old Testament as God-breathed? How can the faith of the Old Testament writers inspire us?

As I have said before, the Old Testament was written over a period of thousands of years. I have said that it is my view that the authors wrote based on their understanding of God at the time that they wrote. So, given the time span, it is reasonable to assume that the various authors will also have had an emerging and slightly different point of view to each other. The text of the Old Testament actually bears that out, giving credence to the view that I've expressed that the text was written based on the authors' understanding of God at the time that they wrote.

The former Archbishop of Canterbury Rowan Williams in his book *Being Christian* says this: 'Did God order or approve of genocide? If He did, that would be so hideously at odds with what the biblical story as a whole seems to say about God. But if we understand that response as simply part of the story, we see that this is how people thought they were carrying God's will at the time.'[5] I couldn't have put it better Your Grace. I believe that's how you address an Archbishop!

By way of an example of this, it's interesting to see the emerging attitude to Gentiles, or foreigners. The book of Joshua describes how the indigenous population were driven from the land promised to them by God. Some Psalms also speak of God giving to Israel the land of foreigners and the fact that families are being driven off land they had farmed for generations doesn't seem to matter.

When the Jews returned from exile in Babylon, some of the surrounding nations offered to help rebuild the Temple. Their offer was refused. Their involvement would render the Temple unclean (Ezra 4: 1-3). Later Ezra realised that members of the Jewish community had defiled themselves by marrying foreign women. It was agreed that these foreign wives were to be sent away. (No mention of how they would survive!)

Compare that with the book of Ruth. She was a Moabitess and after the death of her Israelite husband went back with her mother-in-law to live with her people, the Israelites. She married again, to a Jew and was the great grandmother to David. (Ruth 4:22) Even King David had a Moabitess in his family tree, which means of course, that Jesus did as well, as a descendant of David. Compare that to earlier texts about how foreigners should be viewed. On the face of it, this is an emerging view on the way that God's people should live.

The climax of the Book of Jonah expresses God's love for the people of Nineveh, which He had created in love. (Jonah 4:11). These books are an example of a debate that was going on within Israel about the attitude to those who were not Jews. This journey reaches its climax in the Servant Songs in Isaiah.

'Through you I will make a covenant with all people, through you I will bring light to the nations.' (Isaiah 42:6)

I think that there is another way in which the Old Testament is God-breathed. As you read the Psalms, you explore the vast range of emotions that the writers experienced. They express feelings of worship and love for God, but also sorrow, pain, doubt, guilt, anger and many other emotions. Whatever the emotion you're feeling, the words of the Psalmists can become your words. When you want to cry out to God for help, the words of Psalm 5:2 can become your cry for help. 'Listen to my cry for help, my King and my God, for to you I pray'.

How many countless people of faith have taken comfort from words of Psalm 23 as they near the end of their life? 'Even though I walk through the valley of the shadow of death, I will fear no evil, for you are with me.'

The same can be said about much of the text of the Bible, both Old and New Testaments. They were written in a specific time and place, and yet God can speak through them again and again. And they can do so much more effectively in my view once we free them from a rigid, once-in-time interpretation, which frankly they were never meant to have.

As I conclude this look at the problems I have encountered with the Old Testament, what is my conclusion? I would say that there is a difference between fact and truth. What do I mean by that?

Something may not be factually correct, but there is still truth to be learned from it. If we read the Old Testament from the point of view that it was written by God-fearing people and that what they wrote was based on what they understood at the time they wrote it, then we can learn from it, if we accept that their understanding was not an unalterarable frozen-in-history account.

Their desire was to write about their experience of God, but their views were shaped by the culture of the time that they lived. But things have moved on from then and we can learn from their search for and their relationship with God, if we don't insist on adding to it a requirement that it is truth based on a time frozen in history. God is still revealing new things to us. He does it every day to all of us as we seek Him. If we read the Bible in this way, then it is liberating and we don't tie ourselves up in knots trying to explain the unexplainable.

I have a big plea to my fellow followers of Jesus and it's this. We don't have to agree on everything! Faith is a mystery. God is a mystery. If He wasn't, then He wouldn't be God. We can't understand everything on matters of faith and scripture, and we will come to different conclusions. But my big plea is that we don't discount each other because we don't agree on everything. I may not be right about all my conclusions, but I'm seeking to follow God through Jesus Christ in the power of the Holy Spirit, so please humour me and include me in the fellowship of Christ. I promise to do the same with you.

I'm not pretending that this is the answer to all the questions that anybody may have, but it's a start - at least for me it is. It's not the only difficulty that I have had with faith issues, but I'll move on to those.

Questions to consider

1. Were you aware of these violent passages before reading this chapter? How do you respond to them?
2. Have you ever heard a sermon or attended a Bible Study on the difficult passages mentioned in the chapter?
3. If 'yes', did they honestly explore the problem and were they helpful?
4. If 'no', why do you think these passages are not dealt with in sermons or Bible Studies?
5. What does it mean for you when the Bible is referred to as 'the Word of God'?
6. Can God be violent?

7. How do you reconcile the brutal acts attributed to God in the Old Testament with the nature of God revealed in Jesus?
8. What is your understanding of these words of Jesus, 'You have heard that it was said . . . but now I say to you?'

2

Creation

The earth is a flat disc with the North Pole at its centre and surrounded by an ice wall, which we know as Antarctica. So say the Flat Earth Society, which does indeed put forward the theory that the world is flat. This of course flies in the face of two millennia of collective scientific discovery. Belief that the world is in fact spherical is said to be a conspiracy, put forward by the USA and NASA in particular, which it says has tried to mislead us with pictures of the earth taken from space.

Modern flat earth belief originated with the English writer Samuel Rowbotham (1816–1884). He held that the sun and moon were 3,000 miles above earth and that the 'cosmos' was 3,100 miles above the earth. He also published a leaflet, which argued that 'the Bible, alongside our senses, supported the idea that the earth was flat and immovable and this essential truth should not be set aside for a system based solely on human conjecture.' Lest we should think that such thinking disappeared in the late nineteenth century, consider the case of Mike Hughes, a daredevil and flat-earth conspiracy theorist who, on 24th March 2018, used a homebuilt manned-rocket in an attempt to see for himself if the earth is flat. This failed, but he was killed in an accident on 22nd February 2020 while piloting a flight of his steam-powered rocket in a further attempt to prove that the earth was flat. The accident was caused by failure of the parachute on the vehicle.

We find it difficult to believe that anybody today, in the face of such overwhelming scientific evidence, would hold such views, and indeed put their life on the line in defence of them. It is arguable however that a large body of mainstream Christians do so to this day by discounting the vast majority of scientific thinking about the theory of evolution. The first two chapters of the book of Genesis tell the story about the Creation which, according to chapter 1, is said to have happened over six calendar days with God resting on the seventh. Many believe that this account is factually correct in every respect, based on the infallibility and inerrancy of the Bible referred to in the previous chapter.

But in the first two chapters of Genesis, we have two creation stories and they differ on several crucial points. It is often suggested that there is a conflict between science and the Bible. That is only true if Genesis is seen as a factual account of how the world came to be. Whereas some Christians make that claim, the Bible itself does not. So, there is not one but two creation stories in Genesis and many of the details are not compatible, for example, were man and woman created together or separately? Which was created first, the animals or man? The compiler who put these stories side by side must have been able to see these differences, but he doesn't try some editing to make them fit the same timeline. He doesn't see that there's a problem. But we, or many of us, do seem to see it as a problem.

Added to that, those people would attest to the fact that, based on the timelines and genealogy detailed in the Bible, the Earth is in fact no more than 10,000 years old. This is known as Young Earth Creationism (YEC). I have friends who hold this belief, and can I just say that I fully respect anyone's right to hold such views.

I live in the town of Shrewsbury, which is the home town of Charles Darwin, author of *The Origin of Species* and initiator of the theory of evolution. It is fair to say that Darwin's views are not shared by all Christians, and to the extent that they now are, by the vast majority of scientists, this whole debate has been billed as a conflict between faith and science. I think this it totally wrong. I do not see any such need for conflict between them and being a Christian does not mean that I have to reject scientific thinking and discoveries.

Now I do need to make a confession at this stage. Any reference to my old school reports would not lead you to the view that I can speak about science with any degree of proficiency! I well remember on one occasion, my father taking a rather dim view of my end of term exam results for Physics where I was reported as having got 28% in the exam and was 8th in the class. He took the view that with my 8th place, the exam must have been very difficult. What he didn't know was that the Physics teacher had got the numbers the wrong way around and I didn't think it wise to enlighten him! So, I can't speak with any wisdom on scientific issues.

However, it is evident to me that the vast majority of scientific thinking flies in the face of YEC.

Dr Francis S Collins was head of the Human Genome Project. This was a decade long project to map the DNA of our species, the hereditary code of life. When this project concluded, it was beamed around the world live from the White House, where President Bill Clinton made a speech including these words: 'We are learning the language in which God created life. We are gaining even more awe for the complexity, the beauty, and the wonder of God's most divine and sacred gift.'[6]

In his book *The Language of God* Collins quotes words that he added after those of President Clinton:[7] 'It's a happy day for the World, it is humbling for me, and awe-inspiring, to realise that we have caught the first glimpse of our own instruction book, previously known only to God.' This was from a man who was a rigorously trained scientist, who had moved from atheism to one having a deep personal faith in God. His scientific knowledge led him not to reject the idea of God but to draw him into a deeply held Christian belief.

I am aware of course that YEC proponents can trot out scientists who produce evidence to support their theory, but it has to be said that the vast majority of serious scientific thinking now points to the fact that the earth is around 4.5 billion years old and that life on earth began in its simplest forms about 500 million years ago. As I say, I'm no scientist, but neither am I prepared to just brush this collective thinking aside. To do so I think makes us appear to be ostrich-like in our approach to the whole issue.

In a Gallup poll in the USA in 2004 a question was posed about views on the origins and developments of human beings. The three options put forward were:

1. Human beings have developed over millions of years from less advanced forms of life, but God guided this process.
2. Human beings have developed over millions of years from less advanced forms of life, but God had no part in this process.
3. God created human beings pretty much in their present form at one time within the last 10,000 years or so.

45% chose option 3 and there is little evidence to suggest that this has changed to any significant extent over the past 20 years. It is of course a fact that the USA has a much higher church attendance than the UK, but this statistic is very significant. Whilst the position is slowly changing, there is still an active debate in public schools in America about the teaching of evolution and creationism.

Rachel Held Evans in her book *Faith Unravelled* talks about her school experience. She was educated in Bible Belt country in Tennessee and says: 'Most of my science teachers skipped the chapters on evolution in our Biology textbooks, fearing a backlash from parents.'[8]

Some states are still trying to introduce bills allowing the teaching of YEC as science at the expense of any teaching on evolution.

I'm sure that in the UK a poll of the general population would produce a different result to that in the USA, but if that poll was carried out within Church communities, I do wonder what the results would be.

What of Darwin then? Collins again:[9] 'He proposed that all living species are descended from a small set of common ancestors – perhaps just one. He held that variations in these species occurs randomly, and that the survival or extinction of each organism depends on its ability to adapt to the environment. This he termed natural selection.'

He goes on to say:[10] 'No serious biologist today doubts the theory of evolution to explain the marvellous complexity and diversity of life. In fact, the relatedness of all species through the mechanism of evolution is such a profound foundation for the understanding of all biology, that it is difficult to imagine how one would study life without it.'

So where does that leave us as we read the book of Genesis? If we cannot accept it as a factually correct and scientifically based account of creation, then of what use is it to us as Christians? There is the issue of chapters 1 and 2 contradicting each other as I highlighted earlier. That is only an issue if Genesis is seen as a factual account of how the world came to be. Whereas some Christians make that claim, my belief is that the Bible itself does not make that claim for itself.

My underlying belief is that these stories are of great theological value in their reflection of who made the world and why. But they were not and never intended to be a factual account of how the world came to be. The problem for me and many others is that the those who make claims about the biblical account of Creation being factually correct (YEC) make claims and assumptions that can have the effect of undermining the validity of the faith and belief of those of us who do not share their beliefs.

YEC is commonly now referred to as creationism. However, this does lead to the mistaken belief that those who broadly believe in evolution do not believe in a creator God. This is unfortunate because to assume that acceptance of evolution automatically cuts out God from the process is plain wrong. Darwin himself did not cut God out of the process, in that he did not claim that his findings disproved the existence of God.

YEC holds that evolution is a lie, that each species was individually created by God and that although there may have been some minor changes in species types, each living thing was created individually by God. This includes mankind who it is said was created from dust in the Garden of Eden as depicted in Genesis chapter 2. Interestingly Genesis 1 indicates that God created mankind, male and female together. In chapter 2 it refers to Adam being on his own and God creating Eve out of one of Adam's ribs. YEC believes that Adam and Eve were the first two human beings and that all the rest of the species have descended from them. If the account is factually correct, then there is a fundamental problem here. Chapter 1 and 2 can't both be right in that sense.

I absolutely accept that believers who hold YEC views are sincere believers. So why do they insist on holding views that science has to all intents and purposes disproved? I think part of the reason is that Darwinism has forced them into a position of having to defend God and their faith in Him. If the Bible is to be read literally in all respects, then any theory that suggests otherwise must be refuted.

If we allow these theories to be accepted, then it could be seen to dilute the authority of the scriptures and we are on a slippery slope where anything goes and we are left with nothing. I do think that this argument is understandable, but I believe that the problem disappears if we read the Bible in a different way. If we read the Bible as stories written by people many thousands of years ago based on their understanding of God at the time that they wrote, then we are not forced into mind contortions to justify what we read. Many parts of the Bible were not, in my view, written as eyewitness accounts of actual events. There is much metaphorical writing, storytelling and wisdom-writing at play in its pages.

Just one more scientific argument. Many of the observable stars and galaxies are tens of thousands of *light* years away, and that's just the observable ones. If everything was created no more than 10,000 *calendar* years ago then God is playing a bit of a trick on us!?

There is another concern with YEC. When we put forward arguments that fly in the face of scientific knowledge, we do our faith a great disservice. As we speak about our faith to non-believers, if we seriously ask them to accept YEC, they are likely to reject it and may decide that Christianity is not for them, if they are expected to reject science. Thus, it is not just an issue about what individuals believe - it is an issue about credibility. Francis Collins puts it this way:[11] 'Thus, by any reasonable standard, YEC has reached a point of intellectual bankruptcy, both in its science and its theology. Its persistence is thus one of the great puzzles and great tragedies of our time. By attacking the fundamentals of virtually every branch of science, it widens the chasm between the scientific and spiritual world views, just at a time where a pathway toward harmony is desperately needed.'

So, if people have difficulties accepting YEC, then what are the alternatives? What is it that people can hold onto with a faith that attributes creation to God and yet doesn't dismiss scientific discoveries and truths as something to be just dismissed as irrelevant? Many Christians have found Intelligent Design (ID) to be something that they can accept and which they believe makes science and faith compatible.

William Paley was an English clergyman who died in 1805. Paley used a watch to illustrate his point. He argued that if you came across a mechanical watch on the ground, you would assume that its many complex parts fitted together for a purpose and that it had not come into existence by chance. There must be a watchmaker, or designer. The watchmaker illustration is extensively used by ID followers to illustrate the point.

It is not my intention here to go through the various theories that can be adopted on Creation, but on the face of it this argument deserves some consideration and may even be a compelling argument.

ID has been latched onto by non-scientists to ensure that they can attribute a role to God in the evolution and creation story. Interestingly however the theory attracts very little support in the scientific community. Not surprisingly perhaps, when you consider that the proposition does not come from a scientific background, is not scientifically based, and actually has weaknesses based on the scientific point of view.

ID is at its core a 'God of the gaps' theory. In other words, where we have gaps in our scientific knowledge, then under ID methodology, that gap is attributed to God. The problem here is that those gaps are increasingly being filled. When science fills a gap that was previously unexplained, then those who attached their faith to the ID explanation find themselves backtracking and going on the defensive. This is ultimately what has happened with YEC and even of course the flat earth theory.

So, is there a way that science and faith can be in harmony? Does having a faith in God necessitate us having to ditch any concept that evolution is actually what happened (and is still happening), that natural selection is correct and that Darwin deserves to be accepted or at least not demonised? Does he have to be persona non grata in the Christian community as he appears to be in many Churches? There is another way to consider.

The tentative conclusion that I personally have reached is that evolution is God's way of creating. It is because of this that there is essentially no reason for science and faith to be at odds. It is the basic tenet of my understanding, that God underpins all scientific discoveries and knowledge and there is therefore no possibility that any scientific discoveries will emerge in the future that undermine belief in God. This is commonly referred to as Evolutionary Creation or Theistic Evolution (TE).

I am not on my own in holding this belief which is also endorsed by many prominent Christians including for example the late Pope John Paul II.

TE bases its proposition on the view that the Bible is not a reliable source of scientific knowledge, but it is a reliable source of knowledge of God and spiritual things. So, put simply, the Bible is not a scientific book and was never intended to be one. Looking for scientific evidence in the Bible is simply an irrelevant exercise. Therefore, the accounts in Genesis are about the fact that God created the Earth, *why* He did it, but not *how* He did it. Read in this way, the book of Genesis is an incredible statement about faith in the Creator God.

All kinds of possibilities arise if this basic premise is accepted. Our thinking is limited to space and time, but because God is not so limited, he chose the mechanism of evolution to create the massive diversity of life that we see all around us.

Incredibly of course, God also chose to give rise to special creatures with intelligence and an ability to understand the moral law. He also knew that they would choose to disobey that same moral law. Interestingly, Francis Collins cites C.S.Lewis's writing about the moral law as one reason why he became a believer. Science has no answer to why people choose to act in a moral way when there is no reason to do that which doesn't benefit them or their immediate family or community.

This does not give rise to any incompatibility with science and is compatible with the views of the major monotheistic religions of the world. It does not of course prove the existence of God and cannot, because there is no scientific proof for the existence of God. That requires an act of faith.

Atheists could argue that this is another 'God of the gaps' theory, finding a way to insert God into the equation. The prominent atheist Richard Dawkins has described TE as 'an attempt to smuggle God in through the back door'. But at the end of the day, the truth of this idea can only be tested in our own hearts and minds. But we do not always arrive at the truth by examining what is in our heart and minds. Some issues have to be resolved through logic and rational debate.

By the nature of faith, we do not and cannot know the answers to a lot of these questions. I've attempted here to set out how my thinking has evolved on this whole issue, with the help of others who have thought through and articulated their thinking. What conclusions have I drawn from all this and how can you, as you read this, form your own conclusions? Well, here are a few thoughts of mine.

Do we have to be certain about everything?

Whichever of these ideas we adhere to, or to a mixture of them, can we be absolutely certain that we are right and everybody else is wrong? One of the problems about this whole debate is that people tend to dig in and defend their position at all costs, rubbishing any other view as being plain wrong.

There is no doubt that advocates of a literal interpretation of the Bible were severely rattled by Darwin and have been on the defensive ever since. They are of course not defending themselves - they are defending God, or at least their interpretation of what God actually did. On the other hand, advocates of evolution from the Christian community can be pretty dismissive of those who hold a YEC point of view. One detects a distinct lack of grace in all this! I know that I am as guilty as anybody. It stretches to a lot of other issues as well. I will be writing more about this whole area in a later chapter.

What I am pleading for is that we allow for the fact that I may not be one hundred percent right about everything. Yes, I have a view, but so do you, so do all of us. Let's not appoint Doctrine Police in our churches. Let's discuss and chew over issues of faith and hold our own views lightly, not with a clenched fist. We may actually find that someone else is able to explain their view to us, and it opens things up that we had never considered before.

Peter Enns in his book *The Sin of Certainty* says this:[12] 'When our beliefs are threatened, the instinct, understandably, is to guard them fiercely, to resist any move as long as possible, to make the stress go away, and to stay in the comfort of our familiar spiritual homes. But in resisting, we may actually be missing an invitation to take a sacred journey, where we let go of needing to be right and trust God regardless of what we feel we know or don't know.'

But, you may say, what about all the views you're expressing in this book. Isn't that what you're now asking us not to do? Well, hopefully not. In this book I do accept that I express views, including conclusions that I've reached, but I also cover areas where I admit I don't know, areas where I don't have a total degree of certainty, and am still searching for answers. But whether it's a conclusion or an expression of uncertainty, I'm happy, and I hope prepared to be open and have that conversation.

How to read the Bible

Notwithstanding what I've just said, I think that we have to avoid reading the Bible as a scientific manual. The stories of Creation in Genesis are an amazing piece of writing. They say so much about the wonder of the natural world and the universe. They give amazing insight into God's relationship with us, the pitfalls and the possibilities. They help us to know how to help shape that relationship and they lead us to worship God for what He's done and continues to do.

When we don't have to wrestle with whether the Genesis accounts are factually correct, we are released to see such wisdom and riches in these pages. For example, Genesis says that we are made in the image of God. This opens up such wonders and indeed a great challenge. What does this mean for us as we live out our lives?

It is said that we are given dominion over the animals and charged with cultivating the land, nurturing and caring for it. This has special significance for us in these days as we ponder the harm that we are doing to the natural world. We have been charged with caring for it, but we are doing the reverse. There is a renewed challenge for us here and now, based on ancient scripture.

That is all possible if we can release ourselves from the shackles of having to justify and explain what's written. If we're not trying to defend our position, then we're open to God speaking to us through these passages and the same goes for many other parts of the Bible.

The appreciation of literature, poetry, art and music is optimised when we do just that, appreciate it, rather than analyse it, dissect it and critique it. There is, of course, a place for all of that as well. I'm a great fan of acapella singing in its various forms. But the enjoyment comes not from analysing chord progressions, but by just listening to it and letting the wonder of harmony wash over my senses. The Bible is simply a wonderful book and God can speak to us through it if we let him do so.

Whatever your views, let's agree on one thing... What a wonderful world!

Questions to consider
1. Did you realise that there are two creation stories in Genesis not one? How do we reconcile these two versions of how the world came to be?
2. Are historical events the only form of truth? Can truth be conveyed by metaphor? Is there truth in the parable of the prodigal son?
3. For you, are science and the Bible in conflict?
4. Can Christians who hold different views on evolution and the Biblical accounts of creation live together with respect and love?

3

Does God have a plan for our lives?

A nd does He change his mind from time to time if we pray to Him about it, or others do so on our behalf?

On 11th June 2007 I was admitted to hospital for what was supposed to be a routine medical procedure. By way of background, I have had a cardiac pacemaker since 1991 to treat a condition called Sick Sinus Syndrome. This is a heart rhythm issue and I had started to have blackouts. The pacemaker sorted out the problem, and I had been living with this for sixteen years until an issue arose that led to the need for this particular procedure that I refer to.

I had started to feel unwell and totally lacking in energy. It was discovered that the leads connecting the pacemaker to my heart had become infected. The infection was creeping its way ever nearer to my heart and I was informed that were it to reach my heart it would be fatal. So, the procedure required was to remove the pacemaker leads. This is not normally done as when a pacemaker is changed due to the battery having run down, the leads are left in place. However due to the infection in my case they would have to be extracted.

This proved to be anything but straightforward, and as the leads were being pulled out there was a rupture to my Superior Vena Cava (SVC). The SVC is the large vein that returns blood to the heart and to those with any medical knowledge you will know that rupturing this vein is not a good idea! It is a million miles away from cutting your finger! So, I was bleeding internally and emergency action was needed to repair the vein. There was a cardiothoracic surgeon gowned up and in the operating theatre in case there were any problems. The rupture to the SVC was indeed a very big problem. The surgeon carried out an emergency bypass operation and managed to repair the rupture, before then removing the pacemaker leads. During this time, I lost a large volume of blood, had a cardiac arrest and had to be resuscitated as well as receiving a lot of blood.

Whilst all this was going on Janette was waiting back on the ward and was told I would be in theatre for a couple of hours. When six hours had elapsed, she was naturally getting worried and eventually two surgeons appeared to tell her what had happened. One said, 'I nearly killed your husband and this man saved his life.' She was told that the next few hours would be critical and that in the morning we would know whether there would be brain damage as a result of the extreme trauma.

At this point Janette contacted someone in our Church to ask them to pray for me. The message went around numerous other people who all started to pray. They even interrupted a Church meeting to get everyone to pray. The following morning, I was awoken from an induced coma to find family members around my bed and was asked to squeeze a nurse's finger and wiggle my toes. I was able to do these and this was a sign that, whilst I was still gravely ill, the worst outcome now looked unlikely.

A few days later, the very experienced sister who had been on duty in the operating theatre that day said that she had witnessed two miracles in her career and that I was one of them. She even told me that she had been praying for me the night before the operation. I had never met her before. Even the surgeon who carried out the procedure described my recovery as 'amazing', not language normally used by surgeons. This seemed like an answer to prayer. I certainly thanked God for my miraculous escape from the jaws of death, and have been doing so for the many years since that time.

So, was this an answer to prayer in the strict sense of the word? This is almost going to sound like I am doubting God or being ungrateful for my miraculous recovery. That of course is not the case. But did God directly intervene at that moment and take over to ensure that I didn't die, which to be frank was the most likely outcome of the events as they unfolded. Was my recovery due to the incredible skill of the medical team or was there a miracle? Did God hear the many prayers that were being said and decide that Gareth Evans was due a few more years on earth? Did He hear the pleading of Janette and others, and act to save me? Did He intervene to change the course of events?

If the answer to those questions is yes, then the question arises, why me? Countless prayers are said every day for people who are ill, and so often they appear to go unanswered. People still die, even though prayers are said in faith on their behalf. Why some and not others?

This was one of the big issues that I have thought about a lot in recent years, not just because of my own experience, but also as part of this ongoing reflection about the nature of our faith.

I'm sure that as you read this you can think of people who have been ill and for whom many prayers have been offered asking God for healing. Maybe some have been answered in that the person recovered, but I'm equally sure that many of those prayers will have seemingly gone unanswered and the person died or at least never recovered from their debilitating illness.

St Paul speaks about such a dilemma in one of his letters. It appears that he had some illness that he referred to as a 'thorn in the flesh'. 2 Corinthians 12: 7-9 says that three times he pleaded with the Lord to take it away from him. It is evident from this passage that this prayer was not answered, or certainly not with the outcome that he was looking for. We are not sure what that illness was, but clearly it was affecting him and one would suppose that it may have had a detrimental effect on his ability to carry out his ministry. Would he not have been able to carry out that ministry so much more effectively had God miraculously healed him? What a testimony it could have been to talk about his healing. But no, there was no healing. Paul talks about why that may be in the letter, saying that he believed God to be saying to him that 'My grace is sufficient for you, for my power is made perfect in weakness.'

The Gospels are full of accounts of Jesus healing the sick and even bringing dead people back to life. Not only that, but He told his disciples that they would be able to do the same. John 14:12 records words of Jesus when He told his disciples this, 'Very truly I tell you, whoever believes in me will do the works I have been doing, and they will do even greater things..... I will do whatever you ask in my name.' No ifs and buts about that. If you believe and ask, I will do it. Unfortunately, the reality appears to be that He doesn't and hasn't always done that.

Although the Gospels are full of stories of Jesus' miraculous healings there were still plenty of sick, disabled and gravely ill people left in first century Palestine. Jesus didn't heal everybody there, just a few people had that miraculous blessing. But all those who did come to Him were healed, except in Nazareth because of their lack of faith (Mark 6:6, Matthew 13:58) – which leads on rather neatly to another point.

Some have argued that when prayer is not answered, it is because the person praying doesn't have enough faith. I would not want to be the person to tell someone who has just lost a loved one that they wouldn't have died if they had had enough faith when they prayed. Frankly, it's pretty offensive to suggest that and what picture does it paint of a God of compassion who grants or doesn't grant prayer requests based on the level of faith that they are deemed to have. Then faith becomes a matter of salvation by works – not by grace. Salvation depends on how strong my faith is.

Others argue that the answer they received is not what people were seeking. Maybe the prayer was answered but not in the way that was being sought. Maybe the answer is, not yet.

Of course, it goes beyond matters of illness. People pray about all kinds of things and prayer requests cover a multiplicity of subjects. They can range from wanting a sunny day for the family barbeque to asking God to find them a parking place. And yes, I have heard testimony to the fact that God has found people parking places, has delayed train departures to enable someone to catch it and has changed the weather to accommodate a particular event. These at first sight appear to be pretty trivial. Why would God find somebody a parking place and yet allow a child to die with their whole life before them?

In case anyone is expecting some great revelation at the end of this chapter that explains it all, then I'm afraid you're going to be disappointed. This remains one of the great mysteries of faith. There are no slick answers to these questions, and if we attempt to provide them, then I think we do a massive disservice to many people who have gone through agonies as a result of unanswered prayers and also had severe doubts and even loss of faith because of it.

And yet for all the doubts that we have and the difficulties we face with the whole issue of unanswered prayer, there are instances where it is difficult to provide any other explanation other than that God in some way intervened. Perhaps my own experience is one of those.

I well remember a friend telling me about something that happened to him which can only be described as miraculous. This friend was living in Bristol at the time and one evening he had this overwhelming urge to go to the Clifton Suspension Bridge. He had no need to visit that part of the city, and had not previously had any plans to do so. In fact, it was actually very inconvenient for him to do so at that particular time. Nevertheless, he went there and when he arrived, he came across a young man who had gone there with the intention of jumping off the bridge and was just about to do so. My friend was able to dissuade him from doing it and there is no doubt that his arrival on the bridge at that particular moment saved a life.

My friend was in no doubt that it was God who prompted him to go there. What other explanation could there be other than coincidence?

For all the questions that I may have about unanswered, or seemingly unanswered prayer, I do remain convinced of the power of prayer, because it is so much more than coming to God with a list of requests, albeit in most cases based on genuine needs. We have three wonderful children, but I would be disappointed if the only time that they ever talked to us was when they wanted something. I would certainly want them to talk to us when they wanted something, and I think that is testament to a strong relationship that they would feel able to ask for help, when they needed it. But there is more to our relationship than that. We enjoy their company, and we love spending time with them. That's how it should be in our relationship with God. He isn't just there to grant requests - He wants us to be in a relationship with Him. That is awesome, is it not?!

I know people who are much better at praying than me. It doesn't come naturally to me to spend hours in silent meditation. I wouldn't claim to be a super hero, a spiritual warrior. However, I do believe that there is one way that God does answer prayers. He changes people's hearts and minds. It's said that you should be careful what you pray for, as you may become part of the answer.

As I write this, we are in the depth of a terrible pandemic due to the Covid-19 virus. People have been praying to God to step in and end the crisis, to save lives and to get us back to living normally so that children can get their education, so that people can end their long period of isolation and so that people can go back to running businesses and earning their livings. God doesn't appear to be answering that directly with a miraculous end to the pandemic, but He is answering other prayers:

- He is giving wisdom to scientists as they develop vaccines and treatments.
- He is raising up an army of volunteers to help with the vaccination programme.
- He is inspiring countless community groups to provide practical help to neighbours who are struggling.
- He is giving strength to doctors and nurses to keep going in the face of daunting conditions on Covid wards.

These are all indeed answers to prayers.

But the question remains, does God directly intervene in the affairs of this world? Does He act to cure people? Does He find people a car parking space? Well, if He does, then we must ask again the question that I posed in the beginning. Why sometimes and not always?

Why would God spend His energy on delaying a train so somebody could catch it, but turn his head to the plight of children dying of hunger in many third world countries? Why would He decide to miraculously stop the Covid pandemic and yet do nothing to stop the curse of malaria that kills countless people in tropical countries? Does God only answer the prayers of rich nations?

Surely such a God would be cruel beyond belief. To choose to intervene sometimes and not at others seems unimaginable. There is of course the argument that God has given us free will to make our own decisions in life, and that gives rise to consequences that are sometimes tragic. We all make life choices about whether to smoke, drink and over-eat, and in so doing can give rise to health problems that are a direct consequence of the choices we have made. Sometimes wrong choices have consequences for other people. If a man abuses his wife, then this clearly has direct consequences for her, not of her making and yet she has to suffer as a result.

Why did God allow the horrors of the Holocaust? Why did He allow millions of people to perish at the hands of the cruel and evil Nazi regime?

But not all suffering is as a direct result of the actions of people. What about natural disasters? What about freak accidents? The list goes on.

As Christians we use pictures to paint a picture of God. We say He is a King, almighty and omnipotent. Omnipotent is not a word that is actually used in the Bible, but certainly almighty is. Kings at that time were indeed 'almighty', they ruled as they saw fit and what they said happened. You could not stand up to the power of a King, not that is if you wanted to see tomorrow dawn! This picture implies that God ruled as He saw fit and maybe that's how the people of the time saw God and therefore wrote in those terms.

But the term 'Father' is also used of God and notably by Jesus Himself. Fathers were the head of the household and to some extent therefore they were a bit like Kings, all powerful within their 'kingdom'. Now I know that there are many people who have been scarred by bad parenting and for whom the image of a father figure does not conjure up a positive reaction. But where parenting is seen at its best, it paints a far more effective picture of the divine-human relationship than does kingship. The Bible uses the word 'Father' rather than parent and appears to exclude Mother. However, given the strongly patriarchal nature of society then, this is perhaps not surprising and for our purposes it is much more helpful to use the inclusive term of parent rather than Father. There are however a few examples of female imagery for God. The Spirit of God brooding over the face of the waters (Genesis 1:2), Jesus, longing to mother the people of Jerusalem 'as a hen gather her chicks under her wing', (Matthew 23:37) are two examples.

Dave Tomlinson in his book *Black Sheep and Prodigals* says this: 'The object of any right-minded parent is not to control the lives of his or her children, but to support and empower them to make their own wise and responsible choices in life, to become mature people, decent human beings who can deal effectively with what life presents. And ultimately, parents do not have the power to control what their children will do or become. Parenthood isn't about power, but about love.'[13]

Jesus emphasised this in one of his great parables, the parable of the Prodigal Son. When this young man decided that he had had enough of the parental home, wanted his share of the goodies and split, the father did not stand in his way. He let him go, which allowed him to make some terrible life choices and end up in the gutter. But the father never stopped loving him. He allowed him to make bad choices and he allowed him to suffer as a result of those bad choices. And when the son came to his senses and realised his mistake and went back home, the father was there to greet him with unconditional love. No recriminations, no finger wagging, no price to pay or any hint of punishment, just unconditional love. The father suffered too in this story through the pain of separation. That pain in the heart of God is expressed physically on the cross.

The same couldn't be said of course for his brother who was ready and waiting to dish the dirt, but not the father. There is as much to be learnt from this parable about that brother as there is about the father. Maybe we are all quicker to criticise and point the finger than God is. Food for thought.

So, I'm sure that there is an element of this cause and effect in some of the grief and suffering that we see in our world today. God as a loving Father allows us to make mistakes and allows us to suffer when we make bad choices. He still loves us and of course He calls us to be part of the loving process. We share God's love with those around us who we see suffering. It's one of the amazing ways that God's love is demonstrated, it's not a hands off model, it's a hands on - our hands - model. We are agents of God's love.

But I am certainly not putting this forward as an explanation for all the (excuse this word) shit that goes on. It doesn't help in any way to explain why natural disasters kill so many people in an instant. It doesn't explain why children die at a young age from horrendous diseases. It doesn't explain a hell of a lot to be honest.

Why do these things happen, and does God in some circumstances decide to intervene? I don't know is the honest answer and I'm not going to argue with anybody who feels that yes, God does sometimes intervene and they do indeed have the answer. One of the problems with religious differences and arguments is that some people take up very strong positions and argue strongly from one point of view, to the point where they cannot accept any other point of view. I will come back to this point again later in the book. I believe that we can express a point of view, but accept that others' point of view may have validity. I don't personally think that God finds people parking spaces, but if others believe that He does, then that's fine.

So, did God intervene directly in my life on 11th June 2007? I can't say with certainty whether He did, or He didn't. Whether it was God or the medical team I'm not sure, but whichever it was, I'm eternally grateful that they did and that I've been blessed with more years, years that have seen us be blessed with grandchildren and years of happy retirement. Hopefully there are many more blessings to come, and for them I do thank God.

On a more general level, I think there are two questions that we need to ask. 1) Does God answer prayer? 2) Does God have a plan for our lives? They are clearly not unrelated, but they are two distinct questions. It occurs to me that those who would assert that God answered their prayers are claiming that God altered the original plan.

On the issue of God having a plan for our lives, apart from people who feel called to a particular role, many people talk of things that were 'meant to be', as if there were a higher plan. Some people will say of the person they married, that this was the person they were meant to be with. Some things in life just fit and feel right. We've all had a sense at points in our lives, that this was meant to be. On the other hand, we can see so many things that were clearly not meant to be, that just don't feel right. If we believe God has a plan for our lives, then logically He is responsible for everything that goes on, whether it feels right or whether it doesn't. And clearly, we don't want to say that. And I think we have to say we recognise two realities, which don't fit together in a neat formula and we just have to learn to live with that - two undeniable realities that don't fit together.

But whether God intervenes along the way or not, is there a plan to start with? Does God have a plan for our lives and if so, what is it? And if there is a plan, how do we find out what it is to make sure that we go along with what God has planned for us?

Well, the starting point out for all this is in prayer. Prayer is not just about us asking God for 'stuff' - it's a two-way process. It's said that we can hear God's voice and thus He can tell us what He wants us to do. He can unveil His plan for our lives and then we have to go along with it, if indeed we are truly following God's will for us. Or we can ignore it and basically go our own way, not God's way.

Presumably if God has a plan for some of us, then He must have a plan for all of us. He wouldn't detail how one person is to live their life, but then ignore the next person. And if the plan starts off with the circumstances that people are living in, then it has to be said that for some people it's not much of a plan! If you were a child born in say Sudan, Yemen or Somalia in the current era you would probably have to conclude that it's not what you would have planned. There seems to be a bit of a postcode lottery to all this.

Maybe those children are suffering because of the bad choices that people around them have made and are living with the consequences. Maybe...

But fundamentally does God have a plan, albeit that we have managed to mess up? If we all made right choices and listened to God's voice, then the masterplan would ensure that everything was sweetness and light.

So, if this is all true, how do we hear God's voice? I've heard people say that they have clearly heard God's voice. They believe that God speaks to them clearly and they know what they have to do. For some, that voice is even said to be audible and plain. That is certainly not the case for most of us, but there is clearly a way in which people feel that they can discern God's leading. If you are open in prayer and not just firing off a list of wants, then it's said that God can make Himself known. For others it's an undefined knowing, without being able to clearly articulate how that sense of knowing arises. Pope John XIII used to say that if we live in fellowship with God, we could trust our instincts.

Many people speak of having a sense of calling to follow a particular path in life. They are left in no doubt that God has called them to a particular role, to the extent that some jobs are referred to as a 'calling'. Such jobs would be vicars, pastors, doctors, nurses and the caring professions. People who feel a sense of calling are frequently quite clear that they believe that this is what God wants them to do. I know many such people and I do not doubt their sense of calling in any way.

I do have a bit of a problem though. Why don't many people speak of a sense of calling to be bankers, politicians, journalists, business people, estate agents and accountants? Those who know me well will know that I was a career banker and that my brother was a minister in the Church, so I have a vested interest in trying to understand the answer to this question. Is God really only interested in certain jobs, then calls people into those roles and then leaves everybody else to just get any old job? And then when they have a job, is God more interested in how those people fill their spare time out of work by being involved in ministry within the Church, than He is in what they do whilst they are at work?

By a strange coincidence, my brother, my sister and I all ended up living in Swansea at the same time, where we have no family connections. As my sister put it, my brother was a minister, so he was called to be there. I worked for a bank, so I was sent there. And she was a student, so she chose to go there! Is that the way God works?

It's almost like there is a league table of the spirituality of various roles. Top of the list come vicars, pastors and the like, and then comes caring jobs like medicine and teaching. After that there are social workers and community type caring roles, and then you take your pick after that with the rest.

Does God want people to be bankers, accountants and estate agents? Some would argue that yes He does, because if you are a Christian in a workplace where most people aren't Christian, then you have a chance to be salt and light within those working communities. You can love and care for colleagues and help them with issues of faith. But what about the worth of the actual work? Is God interested in having good accountants? Does God want some people to be bankers?

I would say that yes, He does, and that the reason that we have this secular, sacred divide is because we humans have constructed it to be that way. We've spiritualised certain roles and attributed more worth to them in comparison to other jobs than God does. But did He call me to be a banker? Was it part of His plan all along? Maybe it was, or maybe God lets us decide, be it vicar or solicitor.

So, does God have a plan for our lives? I would say not a detailed plan, but I do believe that God wants the best for His people, and that if we make right choices we are more likely to have good outcomes, which I'm sure He is then pleased about.

So, what's the answer? You decide, and maybe that's just what we all have to do.

Questions to consider
1. Have there been moments in your life when you believe God answered your prayers?
2. Has there been an incident in your life when you think God intervened?
3. How do you reconcile a God of love, who is all-powerful, with the suffering endured by so many?
4. Have there been occasions in your life when something felt right, as if this was God's plan for you?

4

What about other faiths?

This is one of the big questions asked by doubters, strugglers and let's be frank, many followers of Jesus. It is said that we live in a Christian country. The Church of England, our national church, is woven into the fabric of many of our institutions. The monarch is also head of the Church of England and bishops sit in the House of Lords and are therefore part of the fabric of our Government.

After any major incidents or events in the country, the Archbishop of Canterbury will be contacted for a comment or observation. Locally, then it will be the local vicar. Many of our primary schools are affiliated to the Church of England, and members of the local church will have reserved places on the Board of Governors. The institution of the state church is woven into the fabric of our society, even though the reality is that only a small minority of our population consider themselves to be members of it.

Other churches such as Roman Catholics, Methodists, Baptists, United Reformed Church, and many others don't get that kind of official recognition. But leaving that anomaly aside, how relevant is it for the Church to be part of the State governance, given that it is evident that we are not any longer really a Christian country. It is estimated that around 5% of the UK population attend Christian worship on a regular basis, and this continues to decline at a steady rate. In 1980 that figure was 11% so church attendance has more than halved in the last forty years. The average age of congregations is inexorably rising and many, if not a majority, of churches have virtually no children as part of their congregations. At the present rate if nothing changes, the state of organised Christian churches in the UK is facing an uncertain future. This is not a consistent picture across the country, and there are growing churches with active all-age membership. Overall however, it must be recognised that the picture is not rosy!

Whilst a lot of the leavers have drifted away, finding the Church to be irrelevant to their lives, there are also in our country many active congregations of other faiths. We live in a multi-cultural country and that has brought with it a rise in the representation of other faiths. There is an active and vibrant Muslim community together with Seiks, Buddhists, Hindus and many others.

Islam is now the second largest religion in the UK with around 5% of the population in 2018, having risen from 4% in 2011. The largest concentration of Muslims is in London, but nevertheless the comparison with the Christian Church attendance is telling. The numbers who attend church may of course not be the same as those who identify as Christian, but there is undoubtedly a distinct trend in religious adherence which cannot be ignored. Is this something that should concern those of us who identify as followers of Christ? This has raised big questions for Christians as it does of course for the members of those other faiths. We can't all be right, can we? If what we as Christians believe about God, revealed through Christ, is right, then that must mean that every other take on matters divine is wide of the mark.

Well, that's the view that has been taken by many Christians over the years. If we rewind around seventy years in this country, it wasn't an issue that really confronted us much. We were then a predominantly Christian country, and we didn't really come across many people of other faiths. But as we have developed into a multi-cultural society, then we have been forced to face up to the issue, not that it wasn't there before. In the past the question of the validity of other faiths was a somewhat academic issue. Now it has been bought nearer to home. It's on our own doorstep. For some, it's next door...

A verse in Acts 4 reads: 'Salvation is found in no one else, for there is no other name under heaven given to mankind by which we must be saved.' The author of the Letter to the Hebrews wrote: 'Now faith is being sure of what we hope for and certain of what we do not see.' The words 'sure' and 'certain' don't leave much wriggle room, and that is how many people view their faith. They don't leave any room for doubt and make a stand for what they believe in with absolute certainty that they are right in every detail, which means of course that others who don't agree are just plain wrong. This has led to polarisation with an 'us and them' situation. We are right and you are wrong. We have salvation, you do not. We are going to spend eternity in Heaven, you are not. Now I fully accept that polite people try to avoid such stark statements but frankly, many do not.

In his book *Love Wins* the American pastor Rob Bell describes how in his church they had held an art show and had invited members to contribute paintings, poems and other works of art that reflected their understanding of what it means to be a peacemaker. He writes: 'One woman included in her work a quote from Mahatma Gandhi, which a number of people found quite compelling. But not everyone. Someone attached a piece of paper to it. On the piece of paper was written "Reality check: He's in hell"'[14] The reason for that of course was that Gandhi was a Buddhist, and because he had not put his faith in Jesus Christ, then he was excluded and rejected for all eternity not by the Christians who would hold such a view, but by God.

Interestingly Gandhi spent a lot of time studying Christianity, as he did other religions, but was critical of the actions taken by Christian missionaries in India because they combined the medical and educational assistance given with demands to convert to Christianity, or that is at least how he saw it. He was undoubtedly a man who sought peace, including that between people of different religions, and it was the ultimate irony that he was assassinated by a Hindu nationalist.

So, is Gandhi in hell? My response to that would be an emphatic no. But what would be the justification in saying that he is, and am I ultimately compromising my faith by espousing the view that he isn't.

The Gospel of John quotes Jesus on this subject. Chapter 14:6 says this: 'I am the way, the truth and the life. No-one comes to the Father, except through me.' These words are used by those who take a fundamentalist view to make it clear that the only way to a relationship with the Father, that is God, is through Jesus, the Son of God, and that any other way is folly and a blind alley that cannot lead to God. Why? Because Jesus said so. What more do you need? And so, if you are not part of the 'us' who accept that, then you are part of the 'them' who do not. I think it is significant that Jesus here uses the word Father, not God. Perhaps He is not saying no one can know God except through Him, but rather that through Him there is a unique relationship with God, as Father. If we accept the traditional interpretation of that verse, then we must acknowledge that the evidence of scripture (not for the first time!) is not consistent.

Being a Christian in a multi-faith world is challenging. If I am true to my faith does that mean that I must make a stand against Islam, Hinduism, Buddhism, Sikhism, Judaism, and all other religions? Or if I say that all religions are valid and all provide a path to God, then am I undermining my own faith? Is a kind of mishmash of all faiths a valid approach?

Rachel Held Evans in her book *Faith Unravelled* describes seeing a crude home video screened on TV showing a woman in a heavy burqa being led out onto a soccer field in Kabul. It appears that she had been accused of murdering her husband, was forced to kneel, and was executed by a shot to the head. It transpired that her husband had a reputation for abuse, and no evidence had been forthcoming other than a confession obtained by two days of beatings with steel cables. This footage was aired by CNN as part of a campaign to convince the American public of the justification for going to war against the Taliban.

Rachel writes this: 'It was God who ordained that she was born in a third-world country under an oppressive regime. God had all the power and resources at His disposal to stop this from happening, and yet He did nothing. Worst of all, twenty years of Christian education assured me that because Zarmina was a Muslim, she would suffer unending torment in hell for the rest of eternity.'[15] It wasn't enough, it would seem, for her to suffer a cruel death at the hands of her accusers, but she would also suffer for all eternity, decreed so by God.

Is it possible that salvation is all down to a post code lottery? I am a Christian, because of personal experience and choices that I have made, but also heavily influenced by the fact that I was born into a Christian family in what was at the time of my birth a predominantly Christian country. But what if I had been born in Afghanistan, Morocco, or Saudi Arabia? I would almost certainly have been a Muslim. I find it difficult to believe that God would reject me for all eternity based on an accident of birth.

And this argument isn't restricted to different religions. Even within the Christian fold people hold differing views and are divided up into different strands and groupings. Broadly speaking there are three main arms of Christianity. They are Protestant, Roman Catholic and Orthodox. Within the Protestant Church there are multiple denominations ranging from Anglican, Methodists through to Baptists, Presbyterian, United Reformed and various independent groups. There are also churches that you might describe as on the fringe of Christianity, having differing views on issues of doctrine. Here I am thinking of Jehovah's Witnesses, Mormons, Christian Scientists, Unitarian, and many others.

This list is by no means exhaustive but serves to illustrate the point that people who would describe themselves as followers of Christ are divided in many ways. Even within denominations there are evangelicals, liberals, and those between the two. And even in this diversity we get the 'us and them' division.

In 1988, Pope John Paul II addressed the European Parliament. The Rev Ian Paisley, a hard-line Protestant from Northern Ireland, who was an elected member of that austere body, stood up and heckled the Pope, denouncing him as the Anti-Christ. When asked about his comments later he said that the Church of Rome was a 'false Church'. He indicated that the Roman Catholic Church was depicted in the 17th Chapter of Revelation. It really isn't possible to find any more direct way of saying that they are a Church directly opposed to Christ, and hence Paisley's label of the Pope as the Anti-Christ. If you care to read that chapter, you will see what I mean, and included in verse 14 you will find the following: 'They (i.e. the Roman Catholic Church) will wage war against the Lamb (i.e. Christ), but the Lamb will triumph over them because he is Lord of Lords and King of Kings.'

This isn't a polite way of saying I disagree with you on some nuances of theology. It is a total and utter disagreement with anything you say or stand for. And this is between one follower of Christ and another. What hope then for people of another faith completely?

In his book *A New Kind of Christianity* Brian McLaren describes attending a meeting in a small town in England where he was there to address the attendees on the challenges and opportunities facing Christians today in our theology, our church life, and our mission in the world. He was building a reputation as a renowned Christian leader and theologian and his audience included people from many different denominations.

He describes something that was happening outside whilst he was in the meeting. 'I looked out of the window and see four concerned people rushing from car to car in the car park, hurriedly placing papers under the windscreen wipers. The leaflets warned participants about this controversial leader who will speak. He is dangerous, and they say unbiblical.'[16]

Rob Bell had a similar experience when he was addressing a meeting, where those outside were openly protesting against him with placards saying, 'Turn or Burn'. In other words, follow this man and you're destined for Hell!

Now it must be said that hard line outbursts of this nature are not heard very often, and most Christian people are at the very least tolerant of people of other denominations and at best are happy to work alongside them in organisations like 'Churches Together'. But some fundamentalists, if pressed, will say that they do not believe that Christians of a more liberal persuasion have been 'saved', and that they are not going to receive eternal life in Heaven because of their views.

So, this has been a big issue for me and many others to ponder. I do not consider myself to be intolerant, but I do have a strong faith based on my belief that Jesus was and is the incarnate Son of God. Can I reconcile the two?

Part of the problem I think is tied up with the issue of salvation. What is it, and how do you get it? I will explore more of this in the chapter about the Cross which is of course a central part of the Christian faith. Where we find a tension is that if we are truly trying to be followers of Jesus, how can we countenance other faiths having any possibility of really knowing and worshipping God? On the other hand, can I really discount their faith and experiences as irrelevant?

I was very moved to read *I am Malala,* a book written by Malala Yousafzai and which tells her story about how she stood up for education for girls and was shot by the Taliban. At the time she was just a young girl of fifteen, and went on to make a full recovery and continue as an advocate for education rights. She was the youngest ever nominee for the Nobel Peace Prize. What struck me as I read the book is that this was a person who, having a strong faith, knew God in a very personal way. That really shone out of what she wrote about her faith. To quote her: 'I love my God. I thank my Allah. I talk to him all day. He is the greatest.'[17] She is of course a Muslim. What right do I have to say that her experience of the divine has no validity?

Consider the prayer of a Muslim Sufi mystic I came across recently:

My God and my Lord,
eyes are at rest,
stars are setting,
hushed are the movements
of birds in their nests,
of monsters in the deep.
And You are the faithful One,
whose justice never changes,
whose love never grows dim.
The doors of kings are locked,
watched by their bodyguards;
but Your door is open
to all those who call on You.
My Lord, each lover
is now alone with his beloved,
and You are for me the Beloved.
from Muslim Devotions

I think that this is one of the most beautiful prayers I have ever read, and the author clearly has a very deep and personal relationship with God.

As with all the issues that I am addressing in this book, it is possible to come to certain views. I will outline what I see as the possible positions to hold and conclude with the view that I have tentatively come to. I say tentatively because I have concluded that it is wise to hold some of these views lightly rather than grip on for dear life once you've come to an opinion, as someone may tell you something that could persuade you to shift a little in one direction or another.

The first position you can hold is to say that I'm right and anybody else who holds differing views cannot possibly be right or even close to it. Not many of us consider ourselves to be so hard line as this, but I think that there are more people who are basically more fundamentalist than they give themselves credit for. The definition of a Christian fundamentalist is: a person who believes in the strict, literal interpretation of scripture in a religion. A further, more general definition is: a person who adheres strictly to the basic principles of any subject or discipline. That religion, of course, could be any religion, so I do believe that many people take on a fundamentalist view on their faith which doesn't leave any wriggle room when it comes to those who may differ, even marginally. I do not wish to be condemnatory of fundamentalists. People who hold strongly held views and whose faith enables them to live their lives with a certainty of what they believe in, are in many ways to be admired. The problem can arise when that certainty involves discounting any other views as having the possibility of any validity whatsoever.

The first position therefore tends to be intolerant of other views. So secondly, we come to people who take a more open and inclusive view. These people will be happy to have good relations with people of other denominations or even other faiths. They will be happy to give credit to people for the good that they do and perhaps work with them in community projects or inter-faith forums. Their comments will not be derogatory towards others of different persuasion, and they will be happy to engage with them and count them as friends.

But if pressed, those who take this viewpoint may find it difficult to accept that those who take a different view from themselves even have a valid faith at all. This would be much more the case when it comes to other faiths than other Christian denominations, but nonetheless their own personal beliefs and their certainty in their beliefs would ultimately mean that other views aren't right and can't be so. Lovely people and even great friends, they would say, but at the end of the day... wrong.

And so, what of a third option, one which I have arrived at. This all hinges on one or more possibilities:

- What if I'm wrong?
- What if others are right?
- What if we're both right?
- What if we're both a bit right?

Is that possible? Could I countenance the idea that others may have some validity in their faith and that I don't have a monopoly of the truth? Doesn't scripture rule that out? Actually, I don't think that it does. I think the problem is that our tradition has taught us to read scripture in a certain way which fundamentally backs up the doctrine that we've adopted.

This is what David Bentley Hart says in his book *That All Shall Be Saved:* 'I regard the whole process as the unintentional effect of a long tradition of error, one in which a series of bad interpretations of scripture produced various corruptions of theological reasoning, which were themselves then preserved as immemorial revealed truths.'[18]

Is he right? Is it possible that we preserve everything that we have been taught as revealed truth? I said earlier that the evidence of scripture is not consistent. Just consider a few verses that may put a different slant on things. Maybe these are cause for us to re-consider what we have always come to accept:

- I John 2:2: 'He is the atoning sacrifice for our sins, and not only ours but also for the sins of the whole world.'
- Matthew 18:14: 'In the same way your Father in Heaven is not willing that any of these little ones should perish.'

- Romans 11:32: 'For God has bound everyone over to disobedience, so that he may have mercy on them all.'
- John 12:32: 'And I, when I am lifted up from the Earth, will draw all people to myself.'
- 1 Corinthians 15:22: 'For as in Adam all die, so in Christ all will be made alive.'
- Ephesians 1:10: 'This plan, which God will complete when the time is right, is to bring all creation together, everything in heaven and on earth, with Christ as head.'
- Colossians 1:20: 'Through the Son, then, God decided to bring the whole universe back to himself. God made peace through his Son's blood on the cross and so brought back to himself all things, both on earth and in heaven.'

It's worth noting a few things here. These are just a few selected verses, but there are many more that basically say the same thing. Notice the use of the word 'all' in these verses. Not just all who accept certain things or believe in a certain way - *all*. The other thing is that some of these are words of Jesus, not just other writers.

As I said before, this whole issue is tied up with the Cross and salvation, which I will explore more in another chapter. But these verses do suggest that the good news is not just for us but for everybody. At the very least I have drawn the conclusion that it is wrong to claim a monopoly on truth. After all, how can it just be me that is one hundred percent right? Surely it must be right to be open to the fact that I have faith in what I believe, but others have a different faith, and they may be right, or we both may have part of the truth.

There is another concern that I have in making the claim to have a monopoly of truth. Our understanding of God is limited because we only see things through the spectrum of time and space. It isn't possible to have more than a glimpse of the glory of God. If we could fully understand and see God, then he wouldn't be God. It's stating the obvious, but of course God is not limited in the way we are. He is not limited by time and space and therefore knows everything that is going to happen in the future. He knows how things will end. He knows what will happen to each one of us including our eternal destiny. We also know and understand that God loves us. Is it even conceivable that God would create a world in love, knowing that some people would get things wrong in such a way that He would punish them for all eternity?

David Bentley Hart puts it this way: 'If the story really ends as Augustine and countless others over the centuries have claimed it must, with most - or at any rate, very many.... or, really, any.... beings consigned to eternal torment, and if this story then also entails that God freely and needlessly created the World knowing that this would be the result, then Christianity has no good news to impart.'[19]

Rachel Held Evans in her book *Faith Unravelled* says this: 'After we finished the last pages of *The Diary of Anne Frank* in school our teacher informed us that Anne and her sister died of typhus in a prison camp, thanks to Adolf Hitler. I was horrified, not just because of the prison camp but because everything I'd been taught as a girl told me that because Anne was Jewish, because she had not accepted Jesus Christ as her saviour, she and the rest of her family were burning in hell. I remember staring at the picture of Anne on the cover of my paperback, privately begging God to let her out of the lake of fire.' She goes on to say: 'If only born-again Christians go to heaven, then the piles of suitcases and bags of human hair displayed at the Holocaust Museum represent thousands upon thousands of men, women, and children suffering eternal agony at the hands of an angry God. If salvation is available only to Christians, then the gospel isn't good news at all. For most of the human race, it is terrible news.'[20]

I have to say that I find this argument compelling. Why would God do that? Leaving aside the 'eternal agony' aspect, just to be separated from God for all eternity with no possibility of a reprieve don't seem Godlike to me, not the God that I worship anyway.

Now I fully accept that it leaves a lot of questions unanswered and I'm happy or at least content with that. I don't think we need to or can even possibly have all the answers to everything spiritual. So, does that make me a Universalist? Yes, I guess it does, depending on your interpretation of the word universalist. I'm not keen on labels but if that means I believe that all humankind will eventually be saved, then that's a mast I'm happy to nail to my flag to. Universalism from a Christian point of view means that Christ's atonement did in fact atone for everyone's sins. That point of view is not without issues to be debated, and I accept that and am happy to have that debate. Some of that will be discussed in the chapter on the Cross and Salvation.

I believe that many of the problems in our world today, especially those that emanate from a faith perspective, can be traced to intolerance and bigotry. People are prepared to wage war, kill, and even be killed because their views are so entrenched that others who disagree are classed as the enemy. We have seen countless atrocities carried out by Islamic fundamentalists where they are prepared to kill innocent people and even die themselves in the process because they believe they are doing the will of God and will be rewarded in Heaven for their actions. Once I have branded someone as a heretic or an infidel, I am free to kill them.

Our own history as Christians is no better. We have waged war in the name of God. Consider for example the Crusades, where countless numbers were killed in the name of Christ. Was that the will of God? Not by my book and not in my name! If we could learn to adhere to our beliefs and accept that other people have different beliefs and that it is not a matter worth fighting over, then this world would be a far better place. It would also, by the way, be a far better advert for faith, than the example that we set by waging war in the name of religion.

If we go to scripture for our prompting, then as I have said above there are many parts of the Bible which support a Universalist position. Also, the experience and life examples of numerous people of other faiths point to a real and living relationship with and experience of God. There are also many verses which state in quite an unambiguous way that there is only one true way to be saved and that is through Jesus Christ. The truth is you can find a verse to support whatever view you want to take. The crucial point to make is that though there are verses which speak of there being only one way to salvation – through Jesus Christ – there are others (and not just a few) which speak of God's plan to bring all His children home.

The late theologian and Bishop John Shelby Spong said this: 'The older I get, the more deeply I believe but the fewer beliefs I have. When I'm asked to define God, I'm almost wordless.'

So where do we go from here? Is this a plea for tolerance, dialogue, or even shared worship? Is it possible that a Muslim, Jew, or Buddhist could open our eyes to some new aspect of God's being?

Questions to consider

1. Do you have any experience of meeting someone from another faith? What impression did they make on you? Did you recognise in them a genuine relationship with God?
2. How do you think your life might have been different if you had been born in a Muslim country? How would God think of you if you had been?
3. Is the changing balance of religious observance in this country something that concerns you? Are you threatened by living in a multi-faith society? If so, what should our response and actions be?
4. As a Christian, are you open to the possibility of befriending someone from another faith?
5. King Charles once said when he was still Prince, that when he became King he wanted to be '"defender of faith, rather than defender of *the* faith'. What is your view on this statement?

5

The Cross

The Christian faith and our understanding of who God is, is centred on the Cross. That is why, when talking about the Christian Faith, we inevitably get back to the Cross. We think not just about the extraordinary life of Jesus, but His death, the manner of it, and the fact that Christians claim that Jesus rose from death after having been in the grave for three days. Jesus died by crucifixion, executed by the Roman authorities on a wooden cross, a means of execution that they reserved for those who had committed the most heinous crimes, and those that threatened the authority of the Roman authorities.

Such was the manner of His death and the relevance attributed to it, that the Cross has become the symbol of Christianity. Many churches are built in the shape of a cross. They are rotated east to west with the sanctuary, chancel, and altar in the east. This is because the east faces towards Jerusalem, the place where of course Jesus was crucified. People often wear a crucifix as jewellery on a chain or pendant and many buildings including, but not exclusively, churches have a cross prominently displayed.

This is really quite extraordinary when you consider that the cross is a symbol of torture and execution. Imagine if people went around with the emblem of a gallows or guillotine hung around their necks on a pendant! It is unimaginable and yet that is what we do with the cross.

Crucifixion must be one of the most cruel and vile means ever devised by people to carry out the death penalty. During crucifixion, a person was strung up in a way that would strain both the breathing and the circulation. With arms outstretched, a person would have to lift themselves up, in order to breath. Eventually, this would prove too difficult a task, and the person would slowly suffocate on the cross. It is unimaginably cruel and the most dreadful way to die. And yet the Cross, the instrument for carrying this out, is the symbol of our faith and considered the jewellery symbol of choice.

I have tried in this book to highlight some of the issues that cause debate and division amongst Christians, and the Cross is yet another of those issues. Perhaps it is the one that causes the most difficulties, because we are asked to believe that not only did these things happen to Jesus, but that this is the path that God chose and planned to happen, in order in some mysterious way to reconcile Himself with mankind.

So, allow me to reiterate what I said about Jesus' crucifixion in the introduction. Why did it happen and what was God's plan in all this? The basic evangelical take on all this can be summed up as follows:

- God made humans in his own image, but we messed up and sinned big time.
- Because He is a Holy God, He couldn't let all this sin go unpunished, so
- the consequence was eternal damnation.
- The only way to escape this was that someone had to be punished for all this sin.
- God sent Jesus to take the punishment on all our behalf.
- God sent Jesus to the Cross to die instead of us.
- God was satisfied that the penalty had been paid and,
- if we confess our sins and accept Jesus as our Saviour, we are forgiven and
- receive eternal life.

The theological term for all of this is Substitutionary Penal Atonement. For many this is an essential part of their faith, but for many years it was starting to cause me a problem. Would God really do that? Is it actually in His nature to do so? If He tells us to forgive freely, why is He not able to do that Himself?

As I wrestled with this issue, I discovered that the doctrine of substitutionary atonement is one theory about what the cross is all about, but it is not the only one. I discovered that many renowned theologians do not agree with the doctrine at all and believe that the cross can be explained in other ways. I am of course aware that this questioning of substitutionary atonement will cause some to disagree profoundly and indeed be deeply troubled by the suggestion that it is anything else other than the central plank of our faith. I would not wish to offend anybody by the suggestion, but would, in grace, ask those who feel that way to consider the problem that some of us have with the doctrine which, if asked to accept, may be faced with a faith crisis, or even lead to a loss of faith completely.

So having said that, let me outline some of the problems that I have with the doctrine of substitutionary atonement.

1) Jesus teaches us to forgive without limitations. Should God not do the same?

I find it difficult to accept that God would require such a cruel death, or even a death at all in order to be satisfied. Do we really have to believe that God needs to punish us? When my children misbehaved, I was very willing to forgive them.... eventually! If I, as a mortal father, am capable of doing that, is this not something that God our Heavenly Father is also capable of, and indeed willing to do? In Matthew chapter 18 we read these verses: 'Then Peter came to Jesus and asked, Lord how many times shall I forgive my brother or sister who sins against me? Up to seven times? Jesus answered, I tell you not seven times but seventy-seven times.' Jesus was not meaning literally seventy-seven times. What He was meaning is that our forgiveness should be without limit.

If that is what Jesus told us to do, then surely this must be something that God can and does do. I believe that Jesus is saying here that it is the nature of God to forgive. Why then does God require that Jesus die as a punishment for all our sins? Does this not fly in the face of what Jesus said to Peter that day, that we must forgive however many times it takes, when people sin against us?

So, we have to ask the question, is God only willing to forgive because Jesus died on the cross? Did God really need that punishment to take place in order for Him to forgive? I believe that God displays the ultimate act of loving us and that He is able to forgive because that is in His nature to do so. This is not because Jesus was punished in order for Him to be able to give that forgiveness.

2) Is God really that angry, requiring a violent solution to His fury?

And so that leads to the second point which I would I wish to explore. Does this reflect the character of God? In Stuart Townend's song *In Christ alone* there are these lines: 'And on the cross as Jesus died the wrath of God was satisfied.' I have to say that I have great difficulty singing those words - indeed I now remain silent for those two lines when it is sung in church. The idea of an angry God whose wrath is satisfied by the cruel death of anyone, let alone His only Son, is not something that I can readily accept. I'm not saying that love is all sweetness and light and that there is no place for wrath and anger as part of the act of love, but I am not able to accept that it is within the nature and character of God to have His wrath satisfied by the death of an innocent person.

Charles Wesley's famous hymn *And can it be* contains these lines:
'Still the small inward voice I hear,
that whispers all my sins forgiven;
Still the atoning blood is near,
That quenched the wrath of hostile heaven.'

It's a hymn I love singing but those words are rather disturbing as I really pause to contemplate them.

Jonathan Edwards is revered as one of the great American theologians. In his sermon *Sinners in the Hands of an Angry God* he wrote this:

'The God that holds you over the pit of hell, much as one holds a spider, or some loathsome insect over the fire, abhors you, and is dreadfully provoked: His wrath towards you burns like fire; He looks upon you as worthy of nothing else, but to be cast into the fire; He is of purer eyes than to bear to have you in His sight; you are ten thousand times more abominable in His eyes, than the most hateful venomous serpent is in ours. You have offended Him infinitely more than ever a stubborn rebel did his prince; and yet it is nothing but His hand that holds you from falling into the fire every moment.'

Let's be honest, that's pretty scary stuff!

I have benefited from the writings of Dave Tomlinson the vicar, broadcaster and writer. In his book *Black Sheep and Prodigals* he says this: 'I can't for the life of me believe in (much less admire or worship) a God whose anger is quelled by violence and blood sacrifices. How could I revere a God with less virtue, less humanity, than I myself aspire to?'[21]

Steve Chalke in his book *The Lost Message of Jesus* says this: 'John's gospel famously declares God loved the people of this world so much that He gave His only Son (John 3:16). How then have we come to believe that at the cross this God of love suddenly decides to vent His anger and wrath on His own Son? The fact is that the cross isn't a form of cosmic child abuse - a vengeful father, punishing His son for an offence He has not even committed. Understandably, both people inside and outside of the church have found this twisted version of events morally dubious and a huge barrier to faith. Deeper than that, however, is that such a concept stands in total contradiction to the statement, God is love. If the cross is a personal act of violence perpetrated by God towards humankind but borne by His Son, then it makes a mockery of Jesus own teaching to love your enemies and to refuse to repay evil with evil.'[22]

It's fair to say that this book and particularly the term 'cosmic child abuse' landed Steve Chalke in some fairly hot water with some in the church community, but the point is well made. Surely it is not in the nature of God to require such a transaction, in order to forgive. In Jesus we see a reflection of the nature of God and His teaching was that we should love our enemies, forgive and not require an eye for an eye.

3) Are we really saying that we have to do something to make God ready to forgive?

It is without question that at the cross some mysterious and wonderful act of God is at play. I do believe that in some wonderful way God has reconciled us to Himself and that the cross is central to that. We can't earn His forgiveness. That surely is accepted by all followers of Jesus. His forgiveness is absolute and nothing that we can do can earn that forgiveness, nothing! And yet within this doctrine of substitutionary penal atonement we are told that there *is* something that we have to do to earn that forgiveness and salvation, and that is to accept Jesus as our Lord and Saviour. So, there is something that we *are* required to do. In which case forgiveness is conditional on us doing something. That surely is not grace, not as I understand it anyway.

And so tied up with this whole doctrine is a requirement to accept Jesus and to ask forgiveness for our sins. Otherwise, we are told that we are not accepted, and that salvation is not ours. In a previous chapter I quoted from 1 John 2: 2: 'He is the atoning sacrifice for our sins, and not only for ours but also for the sins of the whole world.' That surely means everyone - those who know and accept Jesus, those who don't, and those who have never even heard of Him, let alone whether they have accepted that Jesus died for their sins, have asked forgiveness and are therefore reconciled with God. There is no caveat in that verse - it's absolute. There are many, many passages in the New Testament which say essentially the same thing.

Nobody is beyond God's love and Christians would argue that absolutely anybody, despite how they may have lived or what sins they have committed, has the opportunity to accept Jesus. But the argument is that their forgiveness and salvation is dependent upon them repenting of what they have done and how they have lived. I believe that God's love is bigger than this, that nobody is beyond God's love and that that love is unconditional.

There are other problems associated with the requirement to accept Jesus.

- What about people who have never heard of Him?
- What about people without the mental capacity to do so?
- What about children? Is there a certain age at which children can make that decision for themselves? If so, what is that age?
- For all these people, is there some kind of cut-off point?

To counter these problems, people say that God is just and we can rely on Him to act with justice. I'm sure that is right, but with some of these questions there is the problem of where a line is crossed, particularly regarding people who are considered godless with the crimes they have committed. Could Hitler for instance now be in Heaven? Absolutely not, many would argue, given the enormity of the crimes against humanity that were committed at his instigation. But then we have all sinned to some degree or another. I guess there could be some kind of scale on the severity of sin committed. But where would that cut-off point be between being saved and condemned?

How God forgives was made complicated by teachers at a later stage in the Church's history. We tend to assume that the idea, that on the cross Jesus was suffering to take upon Himself the penalty that should have been ours, has always been the understanding of Jesus's death. But that's not true. It wasn't until the eleventh century that Anselm put forward the theory of penal substitution – that on the cross Jesus became a substitute – taking upon Himself the punishment God required for sin. His ideas were taken up and developed by John Calvin, that the wrath of God was vented on Jesus, so that we could be forgiven and set free from the burden of eternal torment. But as Richard Rohr, the American Franciscan priest said in one of his books: 'That's not forgiveness, that's a deal.'

What we believe is, I think, made of two elements. What is revealed to us in scripture through the guiding of the Holy Spirit is the first, and secondly that which we acquire by being taught it as doctrine by our traditions. What doctrines we accept are largely determined by what tradition we belong to, often born into. And yet so often we cling to these acquired doctrines as if our lives depend on it. And I guess that may be the rub - we think that our lives, our eternal lives, do depend on it.

There is another problem, which may sound somewhat technical, but is still an issue that I feel needs to be addressed. Within the history of mankind Jesus only appeared 2,000 years ago. Countless other people clearly lived before Jesus was born and died. In what way can those people have received salvation if they predate the sacrificial death of Jesus on the cross? It could be of course that, in some mysterious and wonderful way, the timing of Jesus' sacrificial death is not an issue that we should consider. However, I think it is relevant to pose the question. And of course, Jesus died for my sins 2,000 years before I was even born or had committed those sins.

To put this into context, it is worth considering the story of Zacchaeus which is recorded in Luke19. The story recorded there of course outlines that Zacchaeus, when faced with Jesus and the reality of how he had led his life up till then, repented and offered to repay everybody that he had cheated in his life. Luke recalls the words of Jesus when He said: 'Today salvation has come to this house.' But this of course pre-dates Jesus' death on the cross, so how could Zacchaeus receive salvation before the atoning sacrifice of Jesus even took place? Was this in some way the first stage of his salvation?

The case is just one example of the many millions of people who lived before Jesus. These include some of the heroes of faith in the Old Testament such as Abraham, Moses and David. How have they been saved by the atoning death of Jesus thousands of years after they lived and died?

This is also of course all tied up with the whole issue about people of other faiths and no faith at all. We are fortunate of course that whether we are forgiven and accepted by God is in God's hands, not ours. Whatever our views may be, we can surely be confident in a God who is just, fair and loving. What I say on this issue, or indeed what anybody else says, is not really the key issue. The key issue is what God will do Himself.

Why then the Cross?

I appreciate that what I have said up to this point is what I *don't* believe about the cross and salvation. So, what is happening here? What *do* I believe? Why did Jesus die? Did He have to die? And if Jesus didn't die on the cross as atonement for our sins, what was the whole point of it? Did He go through all that for nothing? Here are some thoughts as to how I have come to see the real meaning of the Cross.

1) Jesus us told us not to retaliate or return evil with evil. We see this being lived out on the cross. Jesus refused to retaliate against those who wronged Him. We see in His suffering on the cross the way

God throughout human history has absorbed all the pain and hurt we have inflicted on Him and each other.

For me it is important, in trying to comprehend why Jesus died, to understand the nature of Jesus' ministry. Although He was the Son of God, He did not behave in the way that earthly rulers behaved. To quote Graham Kendrick's worship song, He was the 'Servant King'. His life was based on serving and loving all of mankind. That meant loving people who many considered undesirable and unlovable, namely sinners and prostitutes. Jesus accepted people who were deemed untouchable by the Jewish leaders. He socialised and went to eat in the homes of people who were considered undesirable by the religious leaders of the day.

Jesus' message was always one of non-violence. He told people to turn the other cheek rather than to fight back. And so when it was that the authorities sought the death of Jesus, it was not in His nature to fight back. It was His nature to absorb all the hate and violence which He faced. The Jewish authorities could not accept the way that Jesus challenged the way they did religion. They could not cope with the way that He disagreed with their way of doing things. He was seen as a challenge to their very authority as leaders. And so they sought to get rid of Him.

The criminal who hung beside Jesus on the cross could see that he was paying the price for the way that he had lived, but also recognised that Jesus had a different agenda. He knew that Jesus had done nothing to deserve the fate that had befallen him. The confession of faith by this criminal was a clear vindication of Jesus' non-violent means of establishing the Kingdom of God. In going to the cross Jesus showed that He would not return evil for evil.

Dave Tomlinson again: 'In the cross of Jesus, we see the ultimate expression of divine grace: whatever we do, however vicious, stupid or malicious, God will never stop loving us. The suffering of Jesus is a sacrament of divine love, a powerful means of transforming our lives and the life of the world, not because it pays a debt to God, but because it opens up a different way to be. By absorbing all the violence, personal evil and systematic injustice of the world in the death of Jesus, God invites the world to be saved from itself. Jesus didn't come to change God's mind about us, but to change the way we see and understand God. More importantly it is to change the way we respond to God.'[23]

In any loving relationship the one who loves the most is always the most vulnerable. People often get hurt by people that they love. Jesus is the ultimate example to us of love in action. And so when people turned on Him violently and with hatred, He could do no other than to be vulnerable. This is the ultimate act of love by a loving God.

2) God vindicates Jesus through the resurrection.

And of course, the Easter story is not just about Good Friday. Three days later comes Easter Sunday, when Jesus rose from the dead and showed that all the hatred and violence shown to Him was not the end. In His resurrection Jesus demonstrated that the cross was not His ultimate defeat, but a victory. By conquering death this was the clearest possible way of demonstrating that the Kingdom of God is achieved not by conflict and violence, but by love.

It was not just the Jewish authorities who thought that they had defeated Jesus by crucifying him. His own disciples thought that Jesus had been defeated. They thought that He had been a failure, that the Messiah that they had hoped He would be, had instead been nailed to a cross. On the first Easter Sunday two of Jesus' followers were travelling on the road to Emmaus from Jerusalem and this is recorded in Luke chapter 24 - they were despondent but were soon to meet the risen Jesus. They had no way to explain a crucified Messiah except as a failure, but soon they were to know the reality of a risen Messiah.

Steve Chalke says this: 'What is the meaning of the resurrection? It is first and foremost the validation of Jesus as the Messiah. Through it, Israel's God, the creator, affirms that Jesus really was, all along, His anointed one. The resurrection declares that the cross was the ultimate victory, not a defeat.'[24]

3) Forgiveness isn't cheap. God doesn't just nonchalantly forgive. Forgiveness comes at a cost. That's what we see in the Cross.

We can do no better than to look at Jesus' teaching to find answers to the whole issue of the Cross and why it happened. One of his greatest parables was that of the Prodigal Son. This is the story Jesus Himself told of how God longs to be reconciled to us. At no point does the father seek to inflict retribution against the son. He is overjoyed to see him and when he sees him in the distance, he runs out to meet him. This, says Jesus, is the way God longs to welcome all His errant children home. So why did Jesus have to die? Where is the Cross in this story? When the son leaves home, the father has two choices - to cut the son out of his heart and so spare himself the cost of caring, or he longs in agony for him to return home. There is the Cross - the visible expression of the pain God has been bearing through the centuries because of our sin and disobedience, and the way we hurt each other and ourselves. I love the quotation (I don't know where I read it): 'There was a cross in the heart of God, long before there was one planted on the green hill outside Jerusalem.'

It is also very illuminating to think about Jesus' prayer on the Cross: 'Father forgive them for they know not what they do.' It is a prayer said on behalf of those who have no intention of repenting, but were in the business of crucifying Him. These were people who were most definitely not seeking forgiveness. They thought they had defeated Jesus and silenced Him for good. Are we really to believe that the Father would not have forgiven them because they had not sought repentance? This was the prayer of Jesus at the point of utter desperation and rejection, and yet shows the forgiveness that He sought for those who persecuted Him and totally rejected everything that He stood for. The Cross is not a transaction that secures God's forgiveness. Rather the Cross reveals the forgiveness which was always in the heart of God.

In Helen Waddell's novel *Peter Abelard* there's a passage where Thibault is trying to explain to the young Peter how the cross works. He shows him a tree that has been felled. 'Those rings run up and down the whole length of the tree, but you only see them when it is cut across. That is what the life of Jesus is - the bit of God that we saw.'[25]

I'm not a great fan of labels. We take great delight in labelling ourselves as evangelical, liberal, high, low and various other categories in our Christian faith. People who espouse such views as I have, are often referred to as woolly liberals, and this is not intended as a compliment! I don't think that our cause gets much credit if we attack each other based on our views on this subject. There is more than one way to try to understand what is happening at the Cross, but we need to exercise grace when speaking to each other. We can't be certain what the answer to this theological issue is, but we can seek to demonstrate the grace that Jesus showed.

Ultimately, we see in Jesus one who simply absorbed all the bile and hatred aimed towards Him. His message to 'turn the other cheek' meant that when His life was threatened, He didn't fight back. He absorbed the violence in His own body. It is the ultimate lesson of how to love. Love is giving, not taking. It might seem like defeat at times, but ultimately it's the only way to achieve victory. When we look at the Cross, we see also the Resurrection. The Cross is the vindication that Jesus is the Son of God and that His way is the right way. Act 2:36 says this: 'Therefore, let all Israel be assured of this, God has made this Jesus, whom you crucified, both Lord and Messiah.'

I think that everything to do with Jesus, His birth, life, teaching, death and resurrection should be seen in a way that invites us to live our lives in the way that He lived, to love as He loved, and to become what is possible to be as human beings. Salvation shows us what a life saved in this way looks like.

Questions to consider
1. How do you think of God – an angry God or a God of love?
2. Why do you think so many Christian preachers and teachers focus so much on the anger of God?
3. Think of stories from the life of Jesus where forgiveness is made real. What do these tell us about God?
4. Does there have to be a punishment, or even repentance, before forgiveness can take place? (Remember the father in the prodigal son and Jesus on the cross.)

6

Human Relationships

This book would not be complete without some mention about human relationships and of course that word, sex. Society's view on human relationships and sex has evolved significantly and in recent decades in particular. Same-sex relationships are now considered quite normal in the UK, and partners of the same sex can marry and adopt children without fear of discrimination. That at least is the position in theory, although there is without doubt considerable prejudice not that far below the surface. However, it is also worth remembering that it was only in 1967 that the Sexual Offences Act was passed which decriminalised homosexual acts between consenting males over the age of 21. It was still illegal in Northern Ireland up until 1982.

That is not the case globally, and homosexuality remains illegal in 69 countries around the world. Indeed, in some countries homosexuality is a crime which carries the death penalty. In many parts of the world gay people and those with a sexual identity other than straight continue to be subject to harassment and discrimination.

There has been enormous progress in recognising that sexual identity is not a straightforward issue. LGBTQI+ is now recognised as an evolving way of recognising the different ways that people identify. The acronym stands for lesbian, gay, bisexual, transgender, queer/questioning, intersex. I do not propose to in anyway explore this in detail in this chapter, other than to point out that society does not now officially discriminate against people who identify in different ways. That is not to say that there is not still considerable misunderstanding, bias, and discrimination at large in our society.

Over the years members of the LGBTQI+ plus community have struggled to be accepted within the Church. Many talk of open hostility when they have come out, and there has been without doubt a lack of inclusion and acceptance. So the point is not just how we should view these issues from a moral standpoint, but also how we should treat fellow brothers and sisters in Christ, when they have different views and lifestyles to ourselves.

There is an organisation called *Inclusive Church* whose member churches seek to make clear that they are places where people are welcome, whatever their identity or sexuality. Many Christians have been fearful of joining a church for fear that they would not be accepted and so *Inclusive Church* is a way of letting people know that they will be included and made welcome. It is interesting to note however that there are only three Anglican churches within the whole of Shropshire that are members of *Inclusive Church*. It seems that we can't even bring ourselves to say 'you're welcome'.

This is a multi-faceted issue and I intend to deal with just two issues within this whole arena and they are:
1. The issue of same-sex relationships and marriage as it applies to the people in such relationships.
2. The issue of sex, and whether it should be only within marriage.

Same-Sex Relationships.

Whereas society has moved on in recent times, the question must be asked, has the Church? An additional question of course is, has society been right to move on? Has the Church been right in maintaining the traditional view? People in the UK can now have civil partnerships and marriages, albeit that they are in same-sex relationships. However, this is not universally the case in churches. Much credit must be given to the Methodist and United Reformed Church in the UK who both now permit same-sex marriages within their churches. This is subject to the agreement of individual local churches.

My own Church, the Church of England has not, as yet, made any change to its official doctrine, namely that marriage is only permitted between a man and a woman, and that sex outside marriage is a sin. It is fair to say that there is much debate currently going on, and at the time of writing the Church is undertaking a whole-of-church consultation called 'Living in love and faith'. In doing this, the Church is trying to get the views across the membership of the whole community as to how we should view sexuality, human relationships, and marriage. There remain some very strongly held views, and it is difficult to see how a consensus is going to be reached. There are those within the Church community who are openly living in same-sex relationships, indeed even as ordained priests. Many others within the Church however take a more conservative view and hold that the Church should stick to its current stance on these issues.

Many people who take a conservative view on these matters would argue that it is wrong for the Church merely to change in the same way that society has, and that there should be places where moral standards are maintained and not just changed because society has. This is understandable, but the question is - has the Church been right all along to maintain this moral stand, or has society at large actually got this one right and that we should be inclusive and accepting? Should churches now be places where people can come for their wedding, irrespective of the nature of the partnership and relationship that they are in?

I was very moved to read the story of Vicky Beeching in her book *Undivided*. Vicky is a lifelong Christian and became a household name in Christian music in both the USA and the UK. She has written many well-known worship songs and forged a career as a musician and worship leader in the mega-churches in the USA. She was adored by the evangelical Christian community, but inside she had a real inner battle in that she had known from a very early age that she was gay. Knowing what this would mean if she came out, she kept this to herself until the age of 35 because she feared that, if she were to come out, she would be rejected by the Church community and she would lose everything that she had worked for in her musical career. Eventually she did come out and her worst fears were realised. She was ostracised by the evangelical Church who viewed same sex relationships and homosexuality as a grievous sin.

She had an inner battle for many years as she tried to reconcile who she knew that she was, with the moral view taken by the Church which she loved. This is how she describes the inner turmoil, as she tried to move forward knowing that she was gay, but also convinced that the way she felt was not acceptable to God. She felt this because that is what she had been taught: 'In my anxiety, I created long, detailed prayers that I would recite to myself each time I felt attracted to a girl. It was my own private liturgy, my internal confession booth, in which I told God how sorry I was ten times a day.'[26]

Having read Vicky's book, I must say that I feel a great sense of shame on behalf of the Church because of the way that they treated her and many, many more people like her. Whatever view people take on the moral issue, to treat anybody in the way that she was treated, let alone a fellow member of the Church, is frankly shameful. Even if you take the view that her lifestyle constituted a sin, to treat anybody in this way is not demonstrating the love of Christ. So whatever changes we may make, it goes without saying that we should love and respect each other, irrespective of our differing views or lifestyles.

The question however remains: Are same-sex relationships acceptable to God? To try and answer these questions, we will of course turn to the Bible. As I have said in other chapters, it is debatable whether we can merely use the Bible as a textbook on which the answer to any moral issue can be found by turning to the relevant verse. Those who take the view that homosexuality is a sin, do so by referencing a few verses in the Bible, and there are actually only a few. Here are two quotes from the book of Leviticus:

Leviticus 18:22

You shall not lie with a male as with a woman; it is an abomination.

Leviticus 20:13

If a man lies with a male as with a woman, both of them have committed an abomination; they shall be put to death, their blood is upon them.

These seem pretty straight forward and to the point, and it not easy to discount passages that seem to be fairly clear cut. Are we though to take the whole verse literally? And if we discard one part, what does that say about the authority of the rest of the verse? Not many people who consider same-sex sin to be sinful advocate the death penalty as an appropriate punishment!

However, we also, if we are taking the view that all scripture can be read as clear instructions to us here and now, need to consider the following verse:

Leviticus 19:19 'Obey my commands. Do not crossbreed domestic animals. Do not plant two kinds of seed in the same field. Do not wear clothes made of two kinds of material'.

The Old Testament clearly takes the view that polygamy is acceptable, as is slavery, and of course they were at the time that the Hebrew scriptures were written. I would argue that a developing revelation of God has moved us on from some of the moral standpoints of the Old Testament, and that to use them as chapter and verse to condemn homosexuality is perhaps to misuse scripture. If we are indeed to use the Old Testament as a complete moral guide, then surely it would need to be *all* of it and not selective passages. Nobody would seriously say now that making a garment out of two kinds of material is a sin, so I think we have to be very careful if we just use passages that suit our point of view.

It's worth making the obvious point that if we have come to the conclusion that some of these passages do not apply to us today, why do we insist that the verses on homosexuality still apply? Is this just naked prejudice and homophobia?

Turning to the New Testament, Jesus had nothing whatsoever to say about same-sex relationships, although it is interesting to look at Genesis 2:24, which Jesus quoted in Matthew 19:5: 'For this reason a man will leave his father and mother and be united with his wife.' What does this say about marriage between two men, or two women? Are we to conclude that even though He quoted this verse, but didn't say anything about same sex relationships, that this was not something that concerned Him? I would venture to suggest that that is the case, as had He said anything on the subject, then I'm sure that those who heard Him and later wrote about Him would surely have passed it on. Other writers in the New Testament did however have things to say about it.

Here is St Paul on the subject:

1 Corinthians 6: 9-11: 'Or do you not know that wrongdoers will not inherit the Kingdom of God? Do not be deceived, neither the sexually immoral nor idolaters nor adulterers nor men who have sex with men.... will inherit the Kingdom of God.'

Other passages include Romans 1:27 and I Timothy: 9-10. The problem from my point of view on this is that, as with Old Testament passages, there are views that Paul espoused that we would not endorse today such as:

- The authority of the state as God ordained. Romans 13: 1- 2.
- His anti-Semitic views, an embarrassment in inter-faith dialogue. Romans 11:8
- His attitude to slavery. Ephesians 6 : 5 – 9. Colossians 4:1
- His teaching of the place of women in worship
- a. They should have their heads covered (1 Corinthians 11 : 5 – 16).
- b. They should be silent (1 Corinthians 14:34).
- c. Women were not to teach or have authority. They should learn from the men 'in silence and humility'. (1 Timothy 2 : 8 - 15).

It is unquestionable that there are moral issues where we now take a different view to passages of scripture in both Old and New Testaments. That is not to say that we can just decide what we want, and if it doesn't concur with scripture, just shrug our shoulders and do whatever seems right to us. We cannot on the other hand just stick rigidly to scripture written at a time and place in history.

In his book *A New Kind of Christianity*, Brian McLaren outlines a four-stage process that some people go through when they realise that some of the things they have taken as literal truths in the Bible turn out to be different to reality as we now know it. For instance, the discovery of fossils and carbon dating have cast doubt over New Earth Creation Theory. Slavery, segregation and apartheid and the rights of women to vote and lead in state and church have also now rightly been challenged.

The process goes something like this. Firstly, these people will oppose, condemn, and reject modern thinking on these subjects. Then they will modify and make small concessions. After that, they become silent. And finally, they tolerate and accept modern day thinking.

McLaren then goes on to describe how this pattern is at work regarding sexuality: 'Many of us remember when nearly all conservative Christians said homosexuality was simply a perverted choice and therefore a damning abomination. Then more and more leaders modified their previous view by acknowledging that there is an unchosen orientation at play, orientation being a category completely unrecognised in scripture, by the way. During this stage there was a lot of "love the Sinner hate the sin talk". Initially these Christian leaders asserted that the orientation must be healed through prayer and therapy. But then, when a large percentage of purporting healings proved temporary, religious authorities capitulated and adopted an approach where the orientation must be borne through celibacy. Now some have begun to reduce the vehemence or frequency of their pontifications on the subject, and many have gone silent altogether. During the latency, the abomination-become-orientation is being de-stigmatised, so gay unions are increasingly seen as inevitable in one form or another.'[27]

In my view one, of the shameful chapters in recent history of Christianity has been those who have sought to 'heal' people from homosexuality, and people have undergone prayer and therapy of various types to try and change them from their natural sexual orientation. There has been much harm and pain caused by these practices which are something which I feel the Church needs to lament about. It is not even as if they were very successful. After initially claiming that people had been 'cured', they inevitably reverted to their natural orientation, and those that did not felt scarred and wounded by the whole experience.

Jesus had many run-ins with the Jewish leaders regarding the observance of Jewish law. They had a total obsession with following the rules which they felt put them right with God. So for instance, observance of the Sabbath was sacrosanct, and yet Jesus asked the question was the Sabbath made for people or were people made for the Sabbath. Perhaps we should be asking the same question with regards to marriage and our interpretation of what that should mean.

Is this an absolute unchanging institution? Were people made for marriage or was marriage created for people, perhaps including gay people? We in the Church have become, arguably, a change-averse community, but maybe we are the very people who should actually be catalysts for change in our communities.

Brian McLaren puts it like this: 'As a change-averse community, the Church sees the increasing acceptance of gay people as yet another slide down a slippery slope towards moral relativism and decay. As a change-catalytic community, the Church sees this increasing acceptance as, yet another step up in removing the old dividing walls of Jew/gentile, slave/free, male/female, and so on.'[28]

People who take the conservative view on homosexuality do so and quote biblical texts to support their view. Vicky Beeching, who I refer to earlier, scoured the scriptures searching desperately for a way that she could come to terms with her sexuality. It was in the pages of the Bible that she felt God was speaking to her and saying that He loved her and had made her the way she was.

In her book she describes a passage in the book of Acts (Chapter 10) where Peter had a vision: 'He saw a huge white sheet being lowered down from heaven. On the sheet were all kinds of four-footed creatures and reptiles and birds. As he looked at this bizarre sight he heard a voice saying, get up Peter kill and eat. Peter was shocked because the animals and birds on the sheet were ones prohibited by Jewish law, they were unclean food. Peter prided himself on keeping that law fastidiously, so he replied, surely not Lord. I have never eaten anything impure or unclean. The voice came back with an authoritative reply, do not call anything impure that God has made clean.'[29]

The point of the passage is that previously, Jewish followers of Jesus believed that only Jews were God's chosen people and that the Gentiles were outsiders. This of course was the traditional Jewish view at the time and the new Christians naturally thought the same way. This radical revelation to Peter was that Gentiles, non-Jews, were also welcome in God's Kingdom. This would have been unthinkable. Vicky describes what she felt God was saying to her through this passage: 'God was letting me in on a new perspective, one of radical acceptance and inclusion. Do not call unclean what I have made clean echoed around my head and heart. The person I'd always been, a gay person, was not something to be ashamed of. God accepted me and loved me, and my orientation which was part of His grand design.'[30]

This is yet another example of the fact that reading Scripture is not always straightforward. Sometimes it appears to contradict itself and can also be used to support different sides of an argument.

So, churches are now inevitably having to address the question of whether they can offer same sex partners the opportunity of a marriage in church. Within society of course there is the opportunity for civil partnerships, but same-sex couples are denied the opportunity to take their vows in most churches, which may be very important to them. The term 'partner' is not as powerful, nor does it carry the same significance as 'husband' or 'wife'. Inevitably, if we say to people that civil partnerships are the only options within a Church community context, then we are making gay people feel different by the actions that we take.

Within biblical times, marriage between a man and a woman was the norm, and arguably remains the same today. Whereas it may still be more common, it does not have to be exclusively so.

There is a real issue to be faced when it comes to Christian couples who are in same-sex relationships. For Christian people getting married in church, it is important because they are taking their vows in the presence of God and within the marriage service with its faith context. People in same-sex relationships who are also Christians have also spoken of the need to make their commitment in church and recognised as a marriage being a gift from God. The Church as a community is important from a Christian marriage point of view. If we limit people in same-sex relationships to civil partnerships followed by a blessing in church, then we are treating them differently in denying them the opportunity for a marriage ceremony where they make their vows in the presence of God. The question also has to be asked, if it is allowable to bless a civil partnership in church, then why it is not OK for a full marriage ceremony.

The hurt that we have inflicted on gay people by making them feel different is considerable, and I feel that the time has now come where this wrong needs to be put right. We must now stop labelling homosexuality as some kind of sickness, sin, perversion or unnatural condition, and recognise it as a healthy, natural and affirming form of human sexuality for some people. In 2016, according to figures from the Office for National Statistics, 2% of people identified themselves as being gay, lesbian, or bi-sexual, though it is acknowledged that the true figure is likely to be much higher, on account of many not being ready to acknowledge openly their true sexuality. From my point of view, it's pretty unlikely that God would create a very significant proportion of all humans in a way that was contrary to His will.

Marriage

So, what of marriage, and is sex only permissible within marriage?

The institution of marriage has undergone considerable change. In western society, many couples are marrying much later in life, and also choosing to have children later in life. Many couples indeed decide against the institution of marriage altogether, perhaps choosing a civil partnership or not marrying at all, choosing to cohabit, albeit in many cases in long lasting, loving relationships. Whereas church was long considered the only place to get married, it is now possible to tie the knot in all kinds of establishments licenced to carry out marriage ceremonies. These civil ceremonies now account for 75% of all the weddings that take place in the United Kingdom. Walking down the aisle is no longer to be taken literally, in the majority of cases.

However, within some Christian circles, the pattern is somewhat different, and many decide to marry at quite a young age. The reason for this is that they believe that sex should be restricted to being only within marriage. Sex outside of the bond of marriage is considered by many to be sinful. This is not universally the case and within many churches you will find couples who will introduce their other half to you as their partner rather than their husband or wife. This would have been unthinkable several decades ago where such an arrangement of cohabitation was referred to as 'living in sin'. Heads would have turned, and tongues wagged at the very suggestion that some members of the congregation were cohabiting, rather than being a married couple.

Without doubt, we are living in a time of considerable change and a sexual revolution is taking place. Inevitably, as with other issues, people's point of reference to the moral standards they adopt will be verses in the Bible. And yet, over the time that the Bible was written, we see a considerable change in marriage and sexual relationships. In the Old Testament, polygamy was considered acceptable, and many Old Testament characters also had concubines, which, on the face of it, they did with God's blessing.

Let us take as an example Abraham, the father of the Jewish nation. His wife Sarah was initially unable to have children, and so she gave him her servant Hagar as a concubine, in order to have children that she herself could not at that stage produce. It was quite common in biblical times to have a concubine who would have sexual relations with the husband. In this day and age, when men have a mistress, this is invariably kept secret, and causes considerable hurt if and when the relationship is discovered. In biblical times however the concubine was protected and considered part of the family. For good measure, Abraham also had another wife called Keturah, making three in all.

It was of course a patriarchal society, where women had little if any rights, and were considered chattels of the husband. It could be argued that we still live in a patriarchal society although thankfully much has changed in recent years. In trying to faithfully and accurately follow biblical teaching on marriage, it is inevitable that we pick up the flavour of the patriarchal society that existed when the Bible was written. There is still the danger that we interpret biblical teaching on the role of women in a literal way, and read this as God's desire for them, their role in life and their participation in human relationships.

The Ten Commandments are considered the go-to place in the Bible to get a view on the moral standards to adopt in your life. It is interesting to read, therefore, the verse dealing with coveting, which lists your neighbour's wife as something you should not covet alongside his servants, his ox or donkey and any other belongings he may have. This was clearly written from a patriarchal stance and is indicative of numerous other passages to be found in scripture.

John Shelby Spong the late American Bishop in his book *Living in Sin* describes it this way: 'By godly decree the role of women in the past was clear. She was created for marriage and motherhood. She was to be the keeper of the hearth, the rearer of children, obedient and loyal to her husband. If she did not marry, she was viewed as a failure, called pejoratively an 'old maid' and generally pitied. Before marriage at least in the dominant strand of the social order she was expected to be chaste. The typical male expected his spouse be a virgin at marriage and faithful after marriage. Her goodness and success as a woman were determined by how well she satisfied these expectations.'[31]

But the role of women has changed considerably and, it must be said, for the better. That is at least the case in western society, although sadly not the case in many eastern countries. Women are no longer just considered as child bearers and home keepers, but as equal partners with men in the human race. They have their own careers, their own interests and are very much considered as equal partners in any relationship. This inevitably has had an impact within what has been called the sexual revolution. The expectations of both partners must be taken into account in any relationship, be it within marriage or outside of it.

Some people, who for one reason or another do not marry, feel that celibacy is their only option. Celibacy as a life choice is of course right for some people, but the question remains as to whether there is a binary choice of marriage or celibacy. The traditional moralists would argue that there is that binary choice, but I feel that the time has now come when this is not the case.

The Methodist Church, at the same time as approving same sex marriages, also moved away from a position of condemning as sinful, cohabitation of couples without going through a marriage ceremony. That is to be much welcomed. The position in Christian doctrine largely remains that sex is only permitted within marriage, if it is not to be considered sinful.

It is important for me to say at this stage that what I am talking about here is sex within a committed, loving and long-lasting relationship. The comments that I have made are not in any way intended to relate to casual sex which I believe can be the cause of much hurt and misery. Unwanted pregnancies and problems with sexually transmitted disease can and do result from casual sex. I believe that sex is a God given gift to be enjoyed by people in loving relationships.

So the question remains: Does God bless long lasting loving relationships just because they do not sit under the label of marriage? John Shelby Spong outlines his view in this way: 'I do not believe that sexual morality can, in our day, be defined by, or exhausted in the solitary options of faithful marriage or chaste celibacy. These options might well continue to be the stated ideals, the least complicated standards, and may even possess the greatest potential for fulfilment. But I have known too many non-marital relationships marked by the qualities of holiness to suggest that they are immoral because they are not within the narrow bands of legal marriage.'[32]

I have to say at this stage that I am a great fan and advocate for marriage. I've been happily married for many years and consider myself much blessed to have been so. That is not to say however that this is for everybody. I can only agree with Spong in his observation of having witnessed many loving, long lasting relationships that have been clearly much blessed. Such couples have clearly made a real commitment to each other, and whereas that may not have been through the ritual of a ceremony, religious or otherwise, the commitment is nonetheless evident and much blessed.

Questions to consider

1. What does being inclusive mean to you?
2. Do you have friends who are part of the LBTQI+ community? How do you relate to them?
3. What would your reaction be if your church started conducting same-sex marriages or blessings?
4. Is the Church currently maintaining important moral standards, or failing to respond to where society has moved?

7

Where do we go from here?

In many ways this is the most important chapter in this book. I've tried to outline some of the many problem areas that people have with issues of faith, the many disagreements and different interpretations that have arisen and continue to do so. Throughout history, different peoples have always followed different faiths and disagreed profoundly, often violently. It has been said that religion has been the cause of many wars, and with shame it has to be said, that there is much truth in that opinion. To this day many conflicts around the world can be put down to religion.

You only have to look at our own country and the conflicts between Protestants and Roman Catholics in Northern Ireland to see the profound and very disturbing effect that these conflicts can give rise to. Untold misery, injury, and death occurred as a result of what became known as the 'Troubles'. Although matters have eased somewhat in recent years, there is still a sharp division between the different communities in Northern Ireland. Although one could argue that the issue is not one of faith but more of national identity, the fact remains that the demarcation lines between the two communities are drawn on the issue of faith adherence.

In many parts of the world today there is considerable conflict caused by religion, and this has been going on for many centuries. Conflicts between Catholics and Protestants in the sixteenth and seventeenth centuries resulted in barbaric actions by both sides. In the 1840s, Mormons were subject to expulsion from Missouri and

Illinois. In Afghanistan in recent history, the conflict was caused by the Taliban seeking to impose strict Islamic law. Within the Muslim faith, there are sectarian disputes between Sunni and Shiite Muslims. In the Middle Ages, the Crusades were a particularly bloody episode, whereby the Latin Church sought to recover Jerusalem and the surrounding area from Islamic rule.

In a previous American administration, President Trump imposed a ban on the immigration of Muslims on the pretext that its continuation would have, by definition, given rise to an influx of terrorists into their country.

So, when people argue that much conflict has been caused by religion, it is difficult really to argue against this conclusion. The issue is perhaps what is the difference between religion and faith? When I look at my own Christian faith, it is impossible to imagine that Jesus would have wanted me or my forebears to wage war against Muslims, on the pretext that I was growing the Kingdom of God. Our faith is founded upon the love of God, and yet these actions that I have described show anything but a demonstration of love. It appears to be a total contradiction that someone following a particular faith then turns into an aggressive often violent person, merely to proselytise someone to their faith. It may arise from a passionate adherence to a faith doctrine, and yet the results all too often are tragic.

Although this scenario has existed throughout history, it is also tragically very much the status quo. Is this inevitable, or is there a way that we can move forward, holding different views and yet living together in harmony and love? These are things after all, which all faiths advocate. If so, how are we to achieve this? We may not ourselves resort to aggression and violence but many of us find it difficult to accept the validity of somebody else's views. I do not believe that conflict caused by differing views is inevitable, but in order to achieve harmony, I believe that there are certain things that we need to do, and I will now outline some of these.

None of us can claim to have the whole truth at the exclusion of everybody else.

As human beings we are limited by time and space. The human brain is the most incredible organ. Its powers to control the human body are amazing, and yet as mere people we are nothing compared to God. Even our amazing brains are totally incapable of understanding the magnitude and power of God, and yet so often we try and claim to do so. Because we like to be able to explain everything, in many ways we limit God to what we can understand and describe. In doing so, we sell God short because we're simply not able to comprehend the full magnitude of God.

When we dig our heels in and declare with absolute certainty our knowledge about who our God is, we are bound to fall short, because God, by definition, is beyond our understanding, and we cannot possibly fully comprehend all that there is to know about Him. And yet we still do it, and in so doing belittle or totally write off other people's view of the nature and identity of God.

Although we may not always see it this way, our Christian beliefs are made up of two parts, our faith *in* God and our thoughts *about* God. If we can in some way decouple these two elements, then we go some way to moving forward. Our beliefs form a central part of who we are. They give us a sense of our identity in the midst of difficult lives. We find it difficult to comprehend living without our faith to sustain us, and yet so much of our beliefs are in actual fact doctrines which can differ profoundly between each of us.

When Jesus was asked, what were the most important laws, His answer was, 1) to love the Lord your God and 2) to love your neighbour as yourself. As you read the gospel stories, it seems to me that Jesus had so much more to say about how we live and treat other people, than about following correct doctrine. I'm certainly not saying that doctrine is not important, but what I am saying is that to follow God as shown to us through Jesus, is mostly about how we live and how we treat other people. Worship is not really about following doctrine, it's about loving God and each other.

The conflicts that arise between people of different faiths are invariably about differing doctrines. We appear to have a preoccupation with correct thinking. In *The Sin of Certainty* Peter Enns has this to say: 'Preoccupation with correct thinking. That's the deeper problem. It reduces the life of faith to sentry duty, a 24/7 task of pacing the ramparts and scanning the horizon to fend off incorrect thinking, in ourselves and others, too engrossed to come inside the halls and enjoy the banquet. A faith like that is stressful and tedious to maintain. Moving towards different ways of thinking, even just trying it on for a while to see how it fits, is perceived as a compromise to faith, or as giving up on faith altogether. But nothing could be further from the truth.'[33]

In his later years John Shelby Spong said that when he was asked to define God, he was almost wordless. 'The older I get the more deeply I believe but the fewer beliefs I have', he said. Beliefs are so important to us and there is a huge variety of different beliefs. We cannot all be 100% right 100% of the time and yet amazingly that is what we claim. And when we claim that, we pronounce, implicitly, or even explicitly, that everybody else is wrong. I put it to you that that is a fairly good definition of arrogance. We need to learn how to hold our beliefs lightly. That is not to say that we should hold them less than seriously, but hold them with the grace to accept that our finite minds are not capable of knowing the full knowledge of God, but maybe together, all together, we can have a richer understanding.

Living together in harmony with those who hold different views to ourselves is also an important part of our witness to a world where violence and hostility are the result of people holding varying opinions. That is why the Taizé community was formed of brothers from Catholic and Protestant backgrounds. Brother Roger called it 'a parable of unity'. That is what the whole Christian community is called to be, a parable of unity, made up of people with differing beliefs, yet committed to living together in peace and goodwill to one another.

In an inter-faith scenario, an amazing example is the friendship that existed between The Dalai Lama and the late Archbishop Desmond Tutu. They relished each other's company and collaborated in writing a book together called *The Book of Joy*. This is how the back cover describes it:

'Nobel Peace Prize Laureates His Holiness the Dalai Lama and the late Archbishop Desmond Tutu have survived more than fifty years of exile and the soul-crushing violence of oppression. Despite their hardships - or, as they would say, because of them - they are two of the most joyful people on the planet. In April 2015, Archbishop Tutu travelled to the Dalai Lama's home in Dharamsala, India, to celebrate His Holiness's eightieth birthday and to create this book as a gift for others. They looked back on their long lives to answer a single burning question: how do we find joy in the face of life's inevitable suffering? They traded intimate stories, teased each other continually, and shared their spiritual practices. By the end of a week filled with laughter and punctuated with tears, these two global heroes had stared into the abyss and despair of our times and revealed how to live a life brimming with joy.

Despite inhabiting different worlds and faith traditions - one an Anglican theologian renowned for his fight against apartheid, the other a Buddhist monk and Tibet's exiled spiritual leader - Desmond Tutu and the Dalai Lama are kindred souls. Both men are deeply spiritual. Both carry a history of struggle against authoritarian regimes. Both have oriented their lives toward compassion and care for others. But what seems to bond them most is a playful delight in the world. To each other, they are 'mischievous brothers'. Their friendship was not based on any desire to proselytise the other, just a mutual trust and joyful relationship and desire to make the world a better and more peaceful place.'

It's OK to disagree

So, the last point leads me to say that it's OK to disagree. Unless we adopt an arrogant attitude that I'm completely right and everybody else is completely or at least partially wrong, then it must be OK to say that perhaps we both have a partial sight of the truth. For some people with a very strong faith this is enormously hard to do, because their faith is so strong that to accept that it could even be partially wrong, is unthinkable.

In order to defend the view that I'm completely right, it's very easy to use biblical texts to prove it, as this is of course the Word of God.

As we have seen before though, biblical texts can be confusing and sometimes contradictory and it is so easy to take a point of view and then find the texts that back up what you are saying.

However, if we can be open enough to listen to another point of view, it can be most edifying. We might discover compelling insights that we have never seen before or even have been prepared to consider. My own journey of faith over recent years has been littered with such moments. As I read differing views for example about penal substitution, it led me firstly to consider that my previous view may have been wrong, to actually being convinced of a different point of view. If I had never been prepared to even consider a different angle on that particular issue, then I would have never had the opportunity to change my view. Many would argue of course that I was wrong to change my view, but nevertheless it is a process that opens up the possibility of an emerging and developing faith in God.

Other examples of issues where my view has changed, or is still in the process of change, are how we should view other faiths, salvation and universalism and sexuality. I am at present wrestling with the subject of prayer and how it works. Why is it that our prayers seem at times not to be answered? And of course sometimes on these issues we never come to a conclusion. Nevertheless, it is very edifying to share thinking with others on these matters as we ponder them, to get their views, and try to move forward.

As well as disagreeing, I've reached the conclusion that it is perfectly OK to say I don't know. We don't need to know the answer to everything, indeed we cannot. If we accept that as a starting point, it helps us in our faith journey and opens us up to the possibility of listening to others, rather than shutting them out because they come from a different starting point. However, if we accept that there will be differing views and disagreements, there's one thing that we must do –

Disagree well

The problem with disagreements is that this so often leads to conflict. There is a tendency to get very irritated with people who put forward a different point of view to ourselves. I know that I am particularly guilty of this and can be somewhat dismissive of people who hold a different view to me. As an example of this, I remember feeling totally exasperated with a friend who told me that he thought the aids epidemic was God punishing humanity for homosexuality. It is a view that I profoundly disagree with, but when he made that statement, I remember feeling very indignant towards him. I have no doubt in my mind that he is totally wrong, but he is entitled to his view.

It is part of the nature of disagreement that discussions can get heated, but it is in these discussions that we need to show grace. What is needed is certainly debate and discussion with people who hold differing views, but it should be done with grace, because ultimately neither of us can prove who is right. So, I believe that the way forward is for us to disagree well, be accepting of people with different views to ourselves and to be inclusive.

This may sound a fairly obvious way forward, but it is not easy to achieve. So convinced have people been throughout history of the correctness of their beliefs that they have gone to war and resorted to violence, in order to ensure that their view reigns supreme and beyond question and debate. This process starts with each and every one of us. It starts with me showing grace and being courteous with people who hold different views. This applies not just between denominations and different religions, but also with within individual church congregations. It has been said that the Church of England is a broad church, and in my own church I know that people hold differing views. However, we have a common mission to our community and to each other and we can only do this if we hold disagreements gracefully and adopt a missional way forward notwithstanding our disagreements.

Should we promote our own point of view?
This naturally leads to the whole issue of mission and evangelism. As Christians we are all bound by the Great Commission. Jesus told us to go and make disciples of all nations. These are the closing words of Matthew's Gospel. If we are true to this commission to which we are called, how can we then not promote our own faith, which by definition, must be to the detriment of other faiths. Is it legitimate

to evangelise to Muslims, Sikhs, Buddhists and Hindus because they adhere to a different faith and don't follow Jesus?

This is not an easy question to answer. I have gained so much, possibly everything, from my faith, so why would I not try to ensure that other people have the benefit of following Jesus as I have, given that I know how much this would be to their benefit. Depending on your point of view, it could also involve their eternal salvation. On the other hand, as I have articulated that other faiths are not without genuine validity, what right have I to try and persuade them to change their faith and follow mine?

The first thing that I think is important for us to recognise is that when people convert to Christianity, it is not actually something that we as human beings have done. People do not become Christian because they have been won over by some human argument, rather it is because they have been touched by the Holy Spirit of God. People do not become followers of Jesus because they are persuaded by some theory or argument that is put forward, but rather because they have been drawn into a relationship with God through the person of Jesus who has entered into their lives, and it is the Holy Spirit that does this. It's a heart thing, not a head thing.

Our job as followers of Jesus in this whole process is to come alongside people in love and friendship, and tell people why it is that we have the faith that we do. It is our life experiences and convictions that lead people to open their hearts and minds, not well-reasoned arguments. We are called to come alongside people of all faiths and no faith, and our job is not to badger them into hearing our well-rehearsed arguments, but to share what we believe and why. Equally we need to listen to other people's life and faith experiences, not in any judgmental way waiting to counter the points they make with better arguments of our own, but rather to enter into a dialogue and relationship.

The way in which we have treated mission in the past has been much linked with our colonial past, where exploitation went alongside mission. It's very easy to move to a point of view where we have a sincere desire to save souls for heaven, rather than live out our

Christian lives. We can see people of other faiths as a challenge, rather than an opportunity for dialogue and friendship.

In his book *Why did Jesus, Moses, the Buddha and Muhammad crossed the road?* Brian McLaren has this to say: 'We still cherish our distinctive religious identity, but we abandon religious supremacy. We are converted from hostility, from seeing the other as a threat to be feared, pitied, eliminated or refashioned into our image. We are converting to hosts and guests, practising and receiving hospitality, sharing our treasures as gifts.'[34]

He goes on to say: 'That is a great gift of a multi-faith world to Christians: in challenging us to repent of our clannishness, caste-liness and cultural expectationalism or supremacy, our multi-faith context challenges us to become better, meaning more Christ-like Christians.'[35]

So, what should we do when we meet people of other faiths? I think we should have a dialogue, ask them questions, and show an interest in them. We can then try to find out why they believe what they believe, why they are where they are, and why they stay there. Don't see them as someone you need to win an argument with. Enter their world and invite them to enter yours and do all this in a non-judgmental way. Brian McLaren again: 'That's what I imagine Jesus, Moses, the Buddha and Mohammed would do if they met one another along the road. When we cross the road to meet one another as friends, in some way, perhaps they do too through us.'[36]

I find it very encouraging that there is now a developing dialogue between different faiths. In my own town of Shrewsbury, there is an inter-faith forum who meet on a regular basis to chat, explore faith issues, and to try and be a blessing to our community together. They do this not as an opportunity to proselytise each other, but to simply try and build a dialogue. So, I find it very encouraging that when the former Prince Charles, now King Charles, spoke of the time when he was to become King, he said that he wanted to be not 'defender of *the* faith' but defender *of* faith.

The way that we most effectively share our faith is not by shouting at people on street corners through a megaphone, but by living

Christ-like lives. As James put it in his Epistle: 'I will show you my faith by my deeds.'

When approached in this way, living out our faith does not come in anyway as an obstacle to having dialogue with people of other faiths and no faith. I can be true to my Christian faith without having to see it as a means of contradicting or correcting someone else who has a different faith view. And so, I don't have to see sharing and having a dialogue with people of other faiths as a threat to my own faith, but rather an opportunity to learn and understand a different point of view.

Conclusion

In this book I've tried to articulate some of my thinking over recent years. I have learned much from talking to other people and reading various authors take on things. Sometimes I have come to a conclusion, sometimes I have not, and may perhaps never do so. I'm comfortable with that because I do think that we never stop learning. The revelation of God is not a once and for all occurrence, it's ongoing and in some senses the end of the Bible should finish not with a full stop but a comma. 'The Lord hath more truth yet to break forth out of his Holy Word.' John Robinson said these words to the Pilgrim Fathers as they set sail for America.

I entirely accept that some of the thoughts that I have articulated maybe ones with which you do not agree and that is fine. I am grateful though that you have taken the trouble to read what I've had to say, and it's my fervent hope that all of us can continue to have a dialogue as we continue our journey of faith, not in any way trying to dig our heels in and insist that we're right on everything, but rather in a spirit of grace where we seek to learn from each other.

Inevitably this will sometimes make us uncomfortable and lead us to question things that we have never thought to question before. But I think if we are brave enough to open ourselves up to new truths and new revelations, then I think we can only be the better for it. If we undertake all this in the right spirit, then I really believe that there is no need for any of us in the community of faith to be in conflict.

Rather we should be in dialogue and move together as partners as we seek to serve our various communities.

So, I believe that we still have much to learn and discover. This is an exciting prospect and, whereas it may appear daunting at times, I believe that we should approach it with excitement and a willingness to learn and hear from God. Are we nearly there yet? No, we're not, but let's enjoy the journey together.

Questions to consider

1. In what ways has your faith changed or developed in your Christian journey?
2. How do you relate to people whose views differ from yours?
3. Are you content to say 'I don't know' to certain questions about who God is?
4. Could you envisage yourself belonging to a multifaith discussion group?

Endnotes

The Old Testament

1 Richard Dawkins. *The God Delusion*, p.51

2 Richard Hess. *Tyndale Old Testament Commentary*, p.9

3 Dave Tomlinson. *Re-enchanting Christianity*, p.24

4 Peter Enns. *How the Bible actually works*, p.82

5 Rowan Williams. *Being Christian*, p.28

Creation

6 Francis Collins *The language of God*, p.2

7 Francis Collins *The language of God*, p.3

8 Rachel Held Evans. *Faith unravelled*, p.40

9 Francis Collins. *The language of God*, p.97

10 Francis Collins. *The language of God*, p.99

11 Francis Collins. *The language of God*, p.177

12 Peter Enns. *The Sin of Certainty*, p.16

Does God have a plan for our lives?

13 Dave Tomlinson. *Black Sheep and Prodigals,* p.111

What about other Faiths?

14 Rob Bell. *Love Wins*, p.1

15 Rachel Held Evans. *Faith unravelled*, p.90

16 Brian McLaren. *A New Kind of Christianity*, p.11

17 Malala Yousafzai. *I am Malala*, p.265

18 David Bentley Hart. *That All Shall Be Saved*, p.19

19 David Bentley Hart. *That All Shall Be Saved*, p.167

20 Rachel Held Evans. *Faith unravelled*, p.92

The Cross

21 Dave Tomlinson. *Black Sheep and Prodigals*, p.141

22 Steve Chalke. *The Lost Message of Jesus*, p.182

23 Dave Tomlinson. *Black Sheep and Prodigals*, p.149

24 Steve Chalke. *The Lost Message of Jesus*, p.190

25 Helen Waddell. *Peter Abelard*, p.241

Human Relationships

26 Vicky Beeching. *Undivided*, p.30

27 Brian McLaren. *A New Kind of Christianity*, p.239

28 Brian McLaren. *A New Kind of Christianity*, p.242

29 Vicky Beeching. *Undivided*, p.168

30 Vicky Beeching. *Undivided*, p.171

31 John Shelby Spong. *Living in Sin*, p.43

32 John Shelby Spong. *Living in Sin*, p.166

Where do we go from here?

33 Peter Enns. *The Sin of Certainty*, p.18

34 Brian Mclaren. *Why did Jesus, Moses, the Buddha, and Mohammed cross the road?* p.241

35 Brian Mclaren. *Why did Jesus, Moses, the Buddha, and Mohammed cross the road?* p.243

36 Brian Mclaren. *Why did Jesus, Moses, the Buddha, and Mohammed cross the road?* p.216

Bibliography

Beeching, Vicky. *Undivided*. William Collins 2018

Bell, Rob. *Love Wins*. Harper Collins Publishers 2011

Chalke, Steve. *The Lost Message of Jesus*. Zonderman 2003

Collins, Francis. *The Language of God*. Simon & Schuster 2007

Dawkins, Richard. *The God Delusion*. Transworld Publishers 2006

Enns, Peter. *How the Bible Actually Works*. Hodder & Stoughton 2019

Enns, Peter. *The Sin of Certainty*. Harper Collins 2016

Hart, David Bentley. *That All Shall be Saved*. Yale University Press 2019

Held Evans, Rachel. *Faith Unravelled*. Zonderman 2010

Hess, Richard. *Tyndale Old Testament Commentary*. Inter-Varsity Press 1996

McLaren, Brian. *A New Kind of Christianity*. Hodder & Stoughton 2011

McLaren, Brian. *Why did Jesus, Moses, the Buddha, and Mohammed cross the road?* Hodder & Stoughton 2013

Spong, John Shelby. *Living in Sin*. Harper Collins 1990

Tomlinson, Dave. *Black Sheep and Prodigals*. Hodder & Stoughton 2017

Tomlinson, Dave. *Re-enchanting Christianity*. Canterbury Press 2008

Waddell, Helen. *Peter Abelard*. Collins 1933

Williams, Rowan. *Being Christian*. SPCK Publishing 2014

Yousafzai, Malala. *I am Malala*. Weidenfeld & Nicolson 2013